This book is dedicated to Jim Barrett, whose understanding and support made the development of the Bear Mountain Canoe possible.

— Ted Moores

CANOECRAFT

A HARROWSMITH ILLUSTRATED GUIDE TO FINE WOODSTRIP CONSTRUCTION

BY TED MOORES & MERILYN MOHR

Photography by Jim Merrithew
Illustrations by Ian S.R. Grainge
Line Drawings by Phil Miller
Plans by Ted Moores

© Copyright 1983 by Camden House Publishing Ltd.

ISBN 0-920656-24-2

Trade distribution by Firefly Books, Toronto

Printed in Canada for:
Camden House Publishing Ltd.
7 Queen Victoria Road
Camden East, Ontario
K0K 1J0

Cover: A contemporary woodstrip/epoxy canoe (background) mirrors the lines of its turn-of-the-century forerunner. Photo by Jim Merrithew.

CONTENTS

CHAPTER 1   The Poor Man's Yacht: Craftsmanship & Common Sense   8
CHAPTER 2   The Well-Bred Canoe: Cedarstrip Tradition   10
CHAPTER 3   Anatomy of a Canoe: Essentials of Good Design   20
CHAPTER 4   Pipe Dreams to Paper: Choosing the Right Plan   32
             The Plans   40
CHAPTER 5   Preparations: Setting up the Workshop   54
CHAPTER 6   Material Matters: Machining the Wood   68
CHAPTER 7   Functional Form: Making the Mould   82
CHAPTER 8   The Stripper's Art: Building the Hull   94
CHAPTER 9   Character Development: Installing the Trim   122
CHAPTER 10   Final Details: Adding the Finishing Touches   134
CHAPTER 11   Classic Care: A Guide to Maintenance & Repair   138
SOURCES   143

THE POOR MAN'S YACHT

Craftsmanship & Common Sense

It is not possible to put too much quality into a pleasure craft, or indeed into any craft that floats.

— Walter Dean

He looked more like an exile from the strobe-lit set of a John Travolta movie than a habitué of the dusty interior of a carpentry shop. His adroitness with video arcade joy sticks exceeded his familiarity with disk sanders and circular saws. Among his possessions, the youth had but a solitary woodworking implement: a rubber-handled Canadian Tire hammer.

Little wonder, then, when barely suppressed guffaws greeted his announcement that as a summer project, he intended to convert a ruddy stack of wood strips piled behind his parents' garage into a canoe. The proposed vessel, he claimed, would not merely float but comfortably handle the mean-est rapids. What's more, this thoroughly functional watercraft would inspire praise normally accorded a piece of fine furniture.

With blissful disregard to naysayers, the youth removed the family car to a place under the trees, where it became subject to the whims of passing thunderheads and pigeons. He called in outstanding favours with the next-door neighbours to augment his tool collection. And by the time the first hints of red appeared on the maples, he was enjoying leisurely paddles in his own woodstrip/epoxy canoe. In place of the earlier cries of derision, he was now greeted with: "That belongs in the living room, lad, not on the lake."

What makes this youth's story heartening for anyone contemplating building a woodstrip/epoxy canoe is that he is far from being the least likely would-be boatbuilder to have transformed pipe dreams, eagerness and a healthy dollop of sheer naïveté into a canoe whose classic lines and warm-hued natural wood finish make it as much a work of art as a boat. During the same three months the youth spent bent over the emerging form of his canoe in his parents' Ontario garage, a doctor from Saskatchewan, a septuagenarian in California and a New York State man who was legally blind all proved that anyone who has a dozen spare weekends, about $400 and the req-uisite patience can create his or her own woodstrip masterpiece.

This has been born out by dozens of backyard builders who, like the youth, doctor, septuagenarian and New York State man, constructed woodstrip canoes from kits provided by the Bear Mountain Boat Shop of northern Ontario. Over the past decade, Bear Mountain has earned an international reputation for the quality of its woodstrip canoes, one of which now rests in the boathouse of Prince Charles and Princess Diana — a wedding gift from Canadian Prime Minister Pierre Trudeau.

But such quality does not come cheap. So, as the price of a finished Bear Mountain canoe climbed to

$2,500, the company decided to sell kits to paddlers whose lack of affluence was overcome by their ambition. Those kits (no longer available) contained an instruction manual that became refined and augmented as users contacted Bear Mountain with their suggestions, questions and complaints. The result is this book, which, because of its hands-on origins, has evolved to fit the needs of everyone from the confused amateur looking for a quality canoe at discount-store costs to the experienced woodworker seeking a personal challenge. Each phase of the building instructions begins by outlining sound, basic techniques, then proceeds to include increasingly interesting and intricate variations that add character and style.

But the foundation of all so-called "stripper" canoes, exotic and plain, rests on a substance familiar to the first native practitioners of the canoebuilder's art: wood, unexcelled for its stiffness, strength, buoyancy and striking appearance. Slender strips of cedar, ¼-inch thick and less than an inch wide, are glued together on forms that are fixed at regular intervals on a secure, level base. This provides shape and support for the hull, which is sanded, planed and then sheathed inside and out with fibreglass cloth and epoxy resin. The last step is to trim the hull with gunwales, seats and decks.

As well as containing basic step-by-step, how-to information, this guide also provides detailed explanations, and photographs show how to make professionally perfect moulds, how to create a clear, tough epoxy sheath and how to protect it all with a final, flawless coat of varnish. Woodstrip/epoxy construction becomes not only feasible but also well within the reach of anyone who is the least bit handy with tools. When launching day arrives, the builder will be able to christen a craft that can ride out the heavy seas that pound the Magdalen Islands or confidently challenge the Class IV rapids in the main channel of the Ottawa River. And do it with class.

Because a quality wooden boat begins with fine lines, this guide also includes a primer on canoe design that explains, in simple terms, the interplay between a canoe's form and function. Each curve of a canoe, from keel to sheer, from bow to stern, profoundly affects performance. Understanding these characteristics and how they interact will enable the backyard boatman to construct a vessel that will be as satisfying to paddle as it was to build. To this end, plans for seven canoes are included here. Some, like the Peterborough, Prospector and Sunnyside Cruiser, are original, historic designs. Others are modern and incorporate up-to-date hydrodynamics with time-tested styles. Together, these plans reflect the most popular canoe sizes and shapes and include designs suitable for virtually any waters.

Regardless of whether the backyard builder opts for a historic design or a modern adaptation, he participates in a tradition born in the middle years of the last century, long before the advent of aluminum and plastic construction, when Canada's classic canoebuilders employed ingenuity and artistry to transform native designs into cedarstrip classics. Nurtured in an obscure river valley in eastern Ontario, the skills of 19th-century innovators like John Stephenson, Thomas Gordon and Daniel Herald became known from remote African jungles to the tundra of the high Arctic, making "Canadian" and "Peterborough" synonymous with "canoe."

One reason for this widespread acclaim was that these vessels combined the practical joys of a small, affordable boat with the materials and attention to detail of a sailing sloop appointed with gleaming teak and brass. "A canoe is a poor man's yacht," wrote the well-known paddler George Washington Sears in 1885. "In common with nine-tenths of my fellow citizens, I am poor — and the canoe is my yacht, as it would be were I a millionaire."

Regrettably, these artisans have been denied their rightful place in Canadian and boating history. Their beautiful canoes were all but supplanted by assembly-line products whose form followed not function but the dictates of marketing men and cost accountants. By the late 1960s, the rich tradition of Canada's master canoebuilders was carried on by one elderly man toiling in the obscurity of a Lakefield Ontario marina.

But the past decade has seen a renaissance in canoecraft, sparked by a handful of commercial shops like Bear Mountain and by hundreds of inspired amateurs spurred on by the belief that there is still a place for quality and aesthetics in watercraft. The modern woodstrip/epoxy method they developed is a direct offspring of the cedarstrip construction made popular during canoeing's heyday. The new technique retains the unquestionable beauty of wooden boats, while eliminating many drawbacks of that material: dry rot, excessive weight and constant maintenance. Best of all, from the standpoint of nonprofessional woodworkers, woodstrip/epoxy construction eliminates the need for an elaborate mould and for fastening the canoe's planking to ribs. This, for the first time, places cedarstrip construction within the limited skills and resources of backyard boatbuilders.

Perhaps more important, however, is that woodstrip/epoxy construction is enjoyable. And, although few beginners will be able to produce the sort of artistry that earns berths in royal boathouses, anyone who follows the steps outlined in this guide will receive a thrill that had at one time all but disappeared from marine pursuits: the pleasure of skimming over the water in a masterpiece that is so intimately one's own.

THE WELL-BRED CANOE

Canada's Cedarstrip Tradition

When a man is part of his canoe, he is part of all that canoes have ever known.

— Sigurd F. Olson

To the untrained eye, it is nothing more than a skeletal form with blackened hardwood ribs, the salvaged remains of a boat that has been rotting in some beaver swamp since Queen Victoria's Diamond Jubilee. The setting does nothing to dispel this impression: a dim little garage with greasy windows, a bare concrete floor and sagging racks of milled cedar overhead. Ancient tools clutter a messy workbench, beneath which are piled cans of varnish and paint, dusty and partially buried in waves of sawdust. What appears to be the ribbed relic of a 30-foot-long war canoe dominates the flotsam of what is unmistakably an old man's workshop. Resting beside the century-old boat forms, however, is a gleaming new double-ended rowing skiff that belies the frail, useless appearance of the vintage mould from which it has risen.

The skiff's hull is formed of long, tightly joined, gracefully tapered and curving strips of western red cedar, sparkling with the heads of hundreds of copper nails arranged in dead-even rows along its entire length. Inside, it is held together by a row of delicate half-round oak ribs, running the length of the boat from stem to stern at even two-inch intervals and punctuated by four wide seats fashioned of clear-grained Ontario white cedar. The seats are supported by sculpted mahogany brackets; gunwales of white ash and oak merge smoothly at each end into elegant pointed decks of rich butternut. Finished but for a final coat of varnish, the skiff is stunningly beautiful in the midst of the dingy shop, glittering like a diamond in a coal mine. Obviously, this is not an ordinary boat shop, and this is not an ordinary boat.

The overseer of this place is Walter Walker, a small man with a gentle demeanour, sparkling eyes and precious little to say to the casual visitor. The man is painfully understated, but his hands – big, rough hands for a person of his slight frame – do the talking. They are callused and scarred from 50 years of steady boatbuilding, but the breathtaking skiff is evidence that their movements remain as light and alive as the hands of a young virtuoso. They are the hands of a master craftsman, one who long ago surpassed his teachers and all rivals. They build what many consider to be the finest canoes and skiffs known today, works of art. When these hands are finally folded in retirement, there will be none to replace them.

At the age of 75, Walker can be found on most work days in the crowded little shop tucked behind a marina in the village of Lakefield, Ontario, which, with neighbouring Peterborough, has long been noted as the home of Canada's – and the world's – top canoebuilders. Here in the valley of the Otonabee River, hundreds of craftsmen were once employed to turn out the unique cedarstrip canoes that

were celebrated throughout North America, Europe and the international boating world for their beauty, workmanship and grace in the water.

Anyone who would build a woodstrip canoe today cannot help but gain inspiration from the legacy of the Peterborough and Lakefield canoes that are the unmistakable forebears of all lightweight canoes today.

Their builders, early Canadian craftsmen in a drowsy backwater valley in eastern Ontario, can be credited with starting what can best be described as the Golden Age of the Canoe at the turn of the century. As a floating vessel of luxury, the finely finished cedarstrip canoe – the "poor man's yacht" – was leagues ahead of its competition, perfectly suited to the leisurely ways of quiet lakes and rivers, especially those in central and eastern Ontario that had recently been transformed into affluent cottage country. Water courtship became an institution, with the word "canoe" serving as a staple rhyme for "you" in the lexicon of Tin Pan Alley. One contemporary pundit, speculating as to why so many proposals took place in canoes, thought that a woman reclining in the bow of a canoe presented the image of maximum desirability and the fact of minimum accessibility, which momentarily flummoxed the suitor.

One 1920s' cedarstrip canoe recently restored by Walker bears witness to the extent the craft be-

came refined in its romantic role. It contains a specially moulded seat in the stern for the paddling swain, with a long deck in the bow partially enveloping a virtual throne in which the passenger sat facing the stern, while coyly trailing one hand in the rippling water. Cabinets are built beneath the deck on either side of the foremost seat, one apparently intended for liquid refreshment, and the other equipped with a complicated sliding door that opens to reveal a built-in Victrola.

In crafting a woodstrip canoe today, one takes full advantage of the most modern resins, fibres and finishes that high technology can provide, but at the same time, one must stop and ponder the fact that this design can be easily traced to indigenous Canadians. In the short 125 years that trace the white man's influence on the light canoe, evolution has made it faster, lighter and far more durable, but it has left intact the fundamental elegance of the basic design.

The history of North American plank canoes begins in a dog-eared edition of the Katchewanooka Herald dated 1857 – a handwritten news sheet circulated among the settlers in the colonial Upper Canada clearing known as Lakefield – in which the lead editorial waxed effusive about an upcoming canoe race: "We trust the numerous young men of the clearing will show themselves as invincible at the regatta as they would be no doubt in the case of an invasion."

North America's first recorded canoe regatta had taken place 11 years earlier at nearby Rice Lake, but informal races date from precolonial times in Canada. Native canoeists often tested their paddling speed and skills against one another, and the settlers soon followed suit, staging social gatherings around race days.

The 1857 regatta was the first of what was to become an annual event. Although this was a white man's race, the canoes being used were all fundamentally Indian: dugouts and birchbark canoes. Before the regatta was over, two observers had hatched an idea for a new kind of canoe, a white man's canoe made of basswood planks rather than a hollowed-out trunk or bark. This was the beginning of the Otonabee canoe industry.

By 1857, the dugout canoe had evolved into a surprisingly sophisticated craft in the Otonabee Valley. The first dugouts were made by slowly burning out the inside of a tree trunk, controlling the fire with wet mud and scraping away char until a canoe hull appeared. It was then stretched into a flared shape and fixed permanently with thwarts by filling it with water warmed by hot stones. Such canoes could be bought cheaply from local Indians, but many settlers preferred to fashion their own and quickly became skilled. In the early 19th century, Major Sam Strickland, a brother of Catharine Parr Traill and Susanna Moodie,

reported that his first attempt at a dugout "looked more like a hog trough than a boat." But by 1857, his son George had perfected a new method of making dugouts and constructed his *Shooting Star* within five days to compete in the regatta. It was dramatically lighter and better shaped than its predecessors. There is a dugout canoe probably very much like the *Shooting Star* hanging in the Peterborough Centennial Museum today. With a hull planed to an even half-inch thickness and sophisticated lines, it defies visions of mud-wielding char scrapers. Indeed, it shows all the stylish touches that would later become known as quintessentially "Peterborough."

The time of the first regatta marked a turning point in the history of the Otonabee Valley. Now dammed and placid, the river seems typical of the many small streams that wind through the settled eastern Ontario countryside. But in the early 19th century, when the sisters Traill and Moodie wrote of their arduous lives in the "clearings" of the Otonabee Valley, the river was strewn with rapids and flanked by virgin stands of butternut, basswood and cedar. Peterborough and Lakefield were rough-and-tumble mill towns, and the river was constantly choked with logs driven down from the north country. In the minds of Moodie and Traill's enthusiastic British readers, this was *the* Canadian wilderness.

But by 1857, the settlement had

been completed, the land was clear and the logging business was slowly starting to give way to the manufacturing industries that would permeate Ontario by the turn of the century. And the canoes that had always been part of daily life in the workaday world of the original settlers were being put to new, less utilitarian uses.

By contrast, the Indian birchbark canoe survived the white man's use remarkably unaltered. Even the legendary fur traders, who depended almost exclusively on bark canoes, adopted native construction methods wholesale, content merely to substitute metal for stone and bone tools and to standardize the sizes they built. In part, this was due to the genius of its design and construction, which had been refined over centuries to adapt perfectly to the varied conditions of wilderness travel. Like the log cabin, however, the birchbark canoe played a much smaller role in the lives of the pioneers than our mythology supposes. It was not nearly sturdy enough for the tough life of the clearings; only the pretentious favoured it over the dugout.

At the Katchewanooka regatta of 1857, the two types of canoe competed side by side. George Strickland took all honours in the singles "log" division, but even his elegant *Shooting Star* seemed cumbersome and awkward alongside the light, finely shaped birchbark canoes. Among the shorebound spectators, there were two young men with a

The Bettmann Archive, Inc.

The Indians' birchbark construction was adopted with few alterations by explorers and traders who crossed the continent.

vivid appreciation of that fact: John Stephenson, 27, co-owner of a planing mill across the river from Peterborough, and Thomas Gordon, a Lakefield man three years his junior. As hunting companions and canoeists as well as skilled woodworkers, they were well attuned to any improvements possible in either the heavy dugout or frail bark canoe. Watching the regatta, one, or perhaps both of these young men had an idea. Why not

combine the best features of the refined dugout with the principles of lightweight Indian canoe construction? Instead of hollowing out the basswood trunk for a dugout, why not slice it into thin boards that could be bent and held in place over a skeleton of thin ribs typical of European boatbuilding?

We will probably never know which man took up the challenge and built the first white man's canoe. But it is probable that he did

it in that same summer of 1857, first bending square ribs over an overturned dugout and then nailing three wide basswood planks on each side, joining them at either end with rough-sawn stems and sealing the seams between the planks with square battens on the inside; a crude but historic craft.

Gordon was the first to exploit the invention commercially, quickly establishing the world's first wooden-canoebuilding shop.

The Lakefield Canoe Building and Manufacturing Company, circa 1910, one of the early eastern Ontario canoe factories.

first wooden-canoebuilding shop. But he was also a leading craftsman, a perfectionist with an eye to both beauty and utility. The degree to which the new wooden canoe fulfilled both requirements simultaneously eventually proved to be its greatest legacy, a legacy first intimated as early as 1866, when Gordon won the Prince of Wales medal for craftsmanship at the British Empire Exhibition in London.

Stephenson remained a loner, building canoes freelance with only his son to help and eventually selling his patents and business to a firm that became the Peterborough Canoe Company.

Combining as they did the best qualities of Indian design and fine European carpentry, the new canoes flourished with a kind of hybrid vigour. The wide-board basswood canoe proved as capable an

ally in a summer of hunting and fishing as the dugout had been in the clearings, and within a few years, two other men had joined in the business of making them. They were William English of Peterborough and Daniel Herald of Gore's Landing, on the south shore of Rice Lake. Among them, these four men pushed the refinement of their craft at a remarkable pace, and within 25 years, most of them

were offering what would later be perceived as their crowning glory — the cedarstrip canoe.

The first step was the development of solid moulds to replace the overturned dugouts on which the first hulls were formed. Like the canoes themselves, these moulds are unique in boatbuilding history. Built solidly to shape the thin planks and withstand years of hammering, their service to generations of canoe makers helped preserve the characteristic lines of the Peterborough canoe.

With the moulds in place, two other factors combined to push the wide-board basswood canoe in the direction of the cedarstrip. One was the difficulty of bending the wide planks to conform with the compound lines of the mould. To prevent splitting, and because good-quality wide lumber quickly became scarce, the builders were soon using up to four planks per side. Each plank had to be carefully tapered to follow the narrowing girth of the hull toward its ends, and this was accomplished by the use of patterns that determined the taper of each board as it was sawn to shape. According to Walker, even the best builders of the day botched two or three canoes before they managed to produce accurate patterns for a new mould. Their patience paid off, though, and the use of more planks and more skilful pattern-making combined to make the cedarstrip possible — even though the number of planks quadrupled, the new possible — even though the number of planks quadrupled, the new canoes could be built efficiently because all were preshaped on a single pattern.

The challenge of sealing the seams between the butt-joined planks was another crucial factor in the development of the cedarstrip. The first wooden canoes were sealed with raised battens that were fitted over the seams between planks. This awkward arrangement soon gave way to a system of flush battens running along the entire length of each seam. They were installed first by rabbeting (notching) the inside edge of each plank to half its original thickness. When the planks were joined together, this produced a long, shallow channel centred over each seam. But before they were joined, the planks were fitted with wooden battens that filled the channel and rose flush to the inside of the planking, producing a watertight seal. Flush-batten construction is still used by Walker to build war canoes.

This system in turn led to the metallic flush batten, a canoe-long "staple" of zinc or brass pressed into cuts sliced on each side of a seam. Although they probably cut weight and production time, metallic flush battens did not provide the strength of hardwood battens, so the builders responded by moving the ribs closer together. This new "close rib" design and the practice of rabbeting the edges of the planks eventually became es-

sential features of the cedarstrip.

There were some spectacular innovations within this natural evolution, most notably Stephenson's "Patent Cedar Rib" and Herald's "Patent Cedar" canoes. Both builders aimed to eliminate the ridged interior of the rib canoe. Herald succeeded with an extraordinary craft built with one interior layer of planking butt-joined and running from gunwale to gunwale and another longitudinal layer on the outside. Between them was sandwiched a sheet of waterproof canvas. Stephenson's boat was even more awkward to build. It consisted of a single layer of narrow tongue-in-groove planks running from gunwale to gunwale like ribs, with only a few longitudinal battens inside the hull for support. "A beautiful job but too expensive to build," commented Gilbert Gordon (son of Thomas). "It was built on a special mould, and it had adjusting screws on the ends that fitted on the planking. They put it in a dry kiln. Every day, they took it out and tightened up the screws." Walker remembers builders having to assemble Cedar Rib canoes on special moulds, completely dismantling them to get them off the moulds and then putting them back together again in a special jig. "It was quite a job," he says. Another contemporary observer was more emphatic about the merits of the Cedar Rib: "Some of the mildest-mannered people turned into fiends if they were told they had to build a Cedar Rib."

The almost incredible amount of handwork involved in making these canoes made them impractical for large-scale production, although the master builders of the Peterborough Canoe Company remained skilful enough to build a Cedar Rib for Princess Elizabeth on the occasion of her wedding. But their development gives evidence of the unadulterated ingenuity of the Otonabee builders and the pace with which they strove to perfect the white man's canoe. The cedarstrip was the optimum combination of watertight strength, lightness and beauty. While the cedarstrip was evolving from the native dugout along the banks of an obscure colonial river, the canoe was undergoing a metamorphosis across the Atlantic — started by an English philanthropist named John MacGregor, who had been inspired by the bark-and-skin canoes and kayaks he had seen during his travels in Siberia and Canada.

In 1865, six years after his return to England, he designed what he took to be a facsimile of the native watercraft for his own use. The Rob Roy was 15 feet long, clinker-built with overlapping strakes as in a rowing skiff, topped with long kayak-like decks enclosing a small central cockpit. Sitting on the bottom and propelling himself with a double-bladed paddle, MacGregor set out across Europe on a three-month journey in this strange craft. With him went armloads of religious tracts and a little

Union Jack fluttering on the foredeck. Shortly after his return that fall of 1865, he published *A Thousand Miles in the Rob Roy Canoe on Twenty Rivers and Lakes of Europe*, and in the eyes of the world — if not the Otonabee Valley — the modern sport of canoeing was born. MacGregor's book and its sequels were a tremendous success; the public responded not only by buying them but also by forming canoe clubs of their own and building more decked boats in the style of the Rob Roy. Not everyone was impressed with these craft, however. "It is necessity, not choice or pleasure, which justifies recourse to such an imperfect, unscientific, uncomfortable imitation of the true boat," one anonymous cynic fumed. Even so, MacGregor promoted canoeing aggressively and successfully.

Ironically, MacGregor had his greatest effect in the United States, where genuine native canoes had become rarities and the populace found itself suddenly peaceful, prosperous and suffused with a romantic disposition born in the writings of Whitman and Thoreau. Although they experimented with many novel forms of construction, the Americans essentially adopted the same method as MacGregor for their boats, clinching narrow, overlapping planks on sectional forms and then inserting ribs for stiffness and shape. Among American builders, the most famous was J. Henry Rushton of upper New York State, who refined this somewhat inelegant lapstrake-construction method by feathering each narrow plank in order to reduce the amount it overlapped its neighbour, a technique he borrowed from the builders of the famous Adirondack guideboat. Although Rushton's early boats were still entirely distinct from the wooden canoes of the Otonabee builders, their example quite possibly influenced the final stages of the evolution of the Peterborough cedarstrip.

The evidence for this speculation rests in a mammoth exhibition in Philadelphia, where the Republic was celebrating its centennial in 1876. Somewhere on the 236-acre site, among 60,000 other exhibitors strung out along 72 miles of aisles, were three canoebuilders from the Otonabee Valley: English, Gordon and Herald. Rushton was also there, represented by a display of lapstrake rowboats as well as his first canoes, two Rob Roy canoes that had been paddled to Philadelphia from Louisville, Kentucky. Before the exhibition was over, Gordon had added another gold medal to his growing collection. Soon after, according to his son Gilbert, he built his first longitudinal strip canoe. Is it possible that he found Rushton amid the overwhelming jumble and admired his unusual lapstrake canoes? Their feather-edge lap would have been unfamiliar, but their rib style and placement were identical to his own close-rib metallic-batten canoes. But Rushton's ribs supported two-inch planks that seemingly solved a primary drawback plaguing the wide-board canoe — the inevitable shrinkage and splitting that occurred after exposure to repeated cycles of wet and dry.

The first hard evidence of such a narrow plank appears in the original catalogue of the Ontario Canoe Company of 1883, which grew from Stephenson's cottage industry and eventually became the Peterborough Canoe Company. It refers to a "longitudinal rib" canoe, cousin to the notorious tongue-in-groove Cedar Rib. "These canoes have not been much tried," admitted the catalogue, "but we are confident that we can recommend them to the public." This model quickly disappeared from sight, but soon all the Otonabee builders were offering longitudinal strip models. The difference lay in the method of sealing the seams. The edges of the strips in the new canoes were rabbetted like the planks of the earlier flush-batten canoes, except that the milling was done on opposite sides of each adjoining strip. When joined together, instead of forming a channel to receive a batten, they interlocked, enclosing a shiplap joint. This was the cedarstrip canoe: built the same way as the canoes that Walker builds today.

By the time the wooden canoe had been perfected as the cedarstrip, the Otonabee Valley had completely lost its frontier atmosphere. Peterborough itself had embarked on its own industrial revolution that, by the turn of the century, had altered it from a sleepy Mariposa into a hustling dynamo. Railways were being flung across the countryside with gay abandon, and industrial development was the standard of progress. Any town that had a rail connection and a workforce happily plunged into the tumultuous fray. It was only fitting that local canoe-building should begin to take place in factories that were governed not by builders but by aggressive entrepreneurs. In 1892, the Ontario Canoe Company suffered a fortuitous (some say deliberate) fire that enabled it to expand into a larger, more automated plant and to pursue export sales. Meanwhile in Lakefield, Gordon had taken in a partner with the same aim. Soon his factory was exporting 600 canoes a year to England alone. They were shipped overseas partially disassembled and nested one inside the other. In this manner, as many as seven canoes could be packed into one crate, which was itself built on a canoe mould and shaped accordingly.

In Europe and the United States, where decked, Rob Roy-style racing and sailing canoes remained current coin, the new "Canadian" open canoes made an immediate impression. In 1880, Tom Wallace of Gore's Landing served notice of the invasion by winning the one-mile race at the first annual American Canoe Association (ACA) regatta with a single-blade paddle in an open canoe, "while nonchalantly smoking his pipe and pausing to scoop up a drink of water." Thereafter, the Otonabee canoes continued to surpass the performance of their Rob Roy cousins, while U.S. devotees of the decked craft concentrated on perfecting highly specialized sailing canoes. By 1900, an ACA historian would lament that "those who follow any other branch of the sport but [sail] racing do so in the open Canadian canoe."

The Peterborough canoes were successful partly because of their versatility. They were fast and agile in racing competition, yet equally at home on extended wilderness journeys or afternoon fishing jaunts. Yet what really set them apart were their smooth, sleek cedarstrip hulls and the sophisticated shapes they inherited from their Indian forebears. One gauge of their impact was the quickness with which Rushton developed his own version of the "smooth-skin" hull in order to compete with the Otonabee canoes. Not long after that, he also introduced open canoes to his catalogue, and these are the boats for which he is best remembered today.

Despite their popularity as purely recreational craft, the Otonabee canoes never completely abandoned their true roots as working boats for the bush. In 1893, two 18-foot Peterborough cedarstrips were taken by the Tyrrell brothers on what remains one of the greatest canoe trips ever attempted. Heading north out of Edmonton, the Tyrrells covered thousands of miles in the barren-lands to the west of Hudson Bay, exploring territory never before travelled by white men. "Just after reaching the Athabaska River," reports C.E.S. Franks in *The Canoe and White Water*, "they amazed some Indians by paddling their Peterboroughs in circles around the natives' birchbark canoes. This was a measure of the improvement caused by western craftsmanship." The Tyrrells were forced to abandon their canoes, with regret, on the shore of Hudson Bay.

The Hudson's Bay Company was, in fact, the largest customer of Peterborough freight canoes for many years. These were shipped out of Ontario in the dead of winter and left in caches at the ends of the western rail lines until they could be picked up during the spring runoff. By 1898, the success of these large canoes had prompted the Peterborough company to create a serious oversupply that threatened its already precarious financial stability. The problem was cleverly solved by the company's banker, who loaded the entire inventory onto a westbound freight train and personally sold the lot in Seattle to willing Klondike-bound sourdoughs.

William Ogilvy, Dominion Land Surveyor and first Governor of the Yukon, used a Peterborough canoe in his travels to the northern Pacific coast, as did both the American and Canadian engineers on the

The Bettmann Archive, Inc.

Canoes, despite their utilitarian roots, became a symbol of Sunday leisure. Canoe-golf was one of the more ludicrous canoe crazes of the Twenties.

Alaska Boundary Survey. But perhaps the most exotic journey ever undertaken in a Peterborough canoe took place in South America, when Peterborough's own David Hatton and two anonymous companions motored up the Amazon River in a canoe specially designed to accommodate an inboard motor.

In 1904, the future of recreational small craft was altered irrevocably when Ole Evinrude cre-

ated his first sputtering outboard motor. By this time, Herald was dead, and Stephenson and English had retired. Of the pioneers, only Gordon remained an active physical presence in his boatshop. The U.S. canoe boom had already completely succumbed to the bicycle craze of the 1890s, and over the first half of the new century, the production of the Otonabee canoe factories was increasingly given

over to outboard runabouts. Yet there was no abrupt decline in Canadian canoebuilding, as there had been in the United States.

Actually, as early as the turn of the century, the role of the cedarstrip as a working boat had begun to be undercut by the development of the canvas-covered wood canoe. It was much easier to build, rugged, just as efficient and half the price of a cedarstrip. The painstak-

Canoe racers and admirers, Toronto Island. Circa 1908.

ing hand labour and high level of skill required to build a cedarstrip simply carried too high a price, and as the market for recreational canoes slowly dwindled, so did the production of the Otonabee canoe factories. By the end of World War II, they were producing more runabouts, water skis, paddles and even lawn chairs than canoes. And with the advent of the mainte-nance-free aluminum and fibre-glass boats in the 1950s, the factories' history was completed.

Walker once had two helpers working with him in his Lakefield shop, but when business tailed off, they found other jobs. Now, he is alone, and when he dies, a unique century-old tradition of wooden-boat building will die with him.

But an offspring will survive in the form of the modern woodstrip canoe. Just as racing stimulated the first board canoes, it was racing that rescued the cedarstrip from oblivion and stimulated a return to good design and innovative construction. As the Otonabee factories were folding, competition paddlers in the American midwest were rediscovering the fine lines of vee-bottom Peterbor-ough cedarstrips. They tried to reproduce its shape but, being ignorant of the solid mould, instead used a strongback with sectional forms, one in the centre and two others equidistant from the stems. After the canoe was planked, the hull was inverted with the forms still in it. Ribs were steamed and nailed between the forms which were finally removed to insert the last ribs. The difficulties in achieving true lines must have been considerable with such widely spaced forms, but the move was significant — the solid mould, appropriate for mass production was successfully replaced with sectional forms more accessible to the amateur boatbuilder.

Throughout the late Thirties, Forties and early Fifties, racing paddlers tried to eliminate ribs to reduce weight in the cedarstrip, but it was post-war technology in the form of waterproof glues and fibre-reinforced resins that facilitated the transition from cedarstrip to ribless woodstrip canoes. No longer were the innovations limited to a narrow river valley and a handful of builders who devoted their lives to canoes. The woodstrip/resin canoe emerged simultaneously across the continent, in Minnesota, Quebec and California, with commercial and backyard builders all contributing to its improvement. When magazine articles and a handful of how-to books opened the method to the general public, the posterity of the cedarstrip offspring was assured.

At the hands of literally thousands of serious amateur canoemakers, these new woodstrip/resin canoes have, since the early 1960s, moved slowly toward the method described in this book. The sectional forms have been improved and moved closer together to reproduce lines more accurately. The strongest and lightest combinations of wood, glue, resin and cloth are being discovered after years of experimentation. And most important, builders have learned the hard way that modern technology cannot replace time-honoured boatbuilding basics.

The great boatshops of a century ago are now gone, most of the precious moulds taken to the closest dump, broken up and burned. All we have left are the canoes themselves, which continue to surface through the wooden-boat revival of recent years. A grown-up third generation is lifting grandmother's cedarstrip down from the boathouse rafters and rediscovering the joys of a beautiful, well-built boat.

What cannot be resurrected are the proud men in dusty overalls who put something of themselves into each boat they built, doing their best with the materials and tools at hand, always working toward that elusive perfection in form and function. However the techniques evolve, the spirit of those builders will be preserved wherever boats are built with integrity and respect.

Holding on to the cedarstrip tradition: Walter Walker at work in his Peterborough workshop.

ANATOMY OF A CANOE

Essentials of Good Design

It is doubtful whether any first-class canoe is the result of any one person's study. The builder's shop is the mill, he is the miller. The ideas of others are grists.

— **J.H. Rushton**

One does not have to be a naval architect to understand the basic principles of canoe design. They are relatively simple, yet vitally important – especially to the builder.

The curves of a well-designed canoe are its calling card – a proclamation of the kind of paddling it does best. At one time, the lines of the slender, double-ended craft were directly traceable to a particular locale or people. The curious profile of a Newfoundland Beothuk canoe was a far cry aesthetically, functionally and geographically from the sturgeon-nosed craft of British Columbia's Kootenay people. Within the limits of materials and technology, both Indian and early white canoes were traditionally shaped to conform to the kind of waters they plied and to the job they had to do. But with the advent of mass production, that discipline has been lost. In the past 30 years, canoes have more often been designed to conform to the demands of materials rather than function, with efficiency in the water taking a back seat to efficiency in the factory. In building your own canoe, you can shift the emphasis back to performance and rediscover that perfect harmony among canoe, paddler and water.

There is no point in expending so much energy to build a craft that is going to paddle like a barge. At the same time, every builder, designer and paddler has his own version of the perfect canoe. The following section bares my personal biases; you can find others by referring to the books listed in the Sources. The key to sorting through the maze is to determine what you expect of your canoe. Where will you most often paddle, for how long and with what gear? Most paddlers face a range of circumstances. The challenge is to select a design that meets most needs, most of the time.

If your experience in canoes is limited, go to the water to test these principles where it really counts. Examine hull contours and paddle different canoes to discover what suits your style best. Your wood-strip canoe will be a thing of aesthetic beauty, but understanding design will assure that it is satisfyingly functional as well.

A Canoe in Perspective

When a canoe is taken out of its watery element and projected onto a drawing board, it can be reduced to three views – profile, body plan and plan view.

The *profile view* (illustrated on page 23) shows a canoe from one side, as if it were cut in half lengthwise. This perspective describes the accurate length and depth of the boat, its sheer-line (the curve of the gunwale or top edge), its keel-

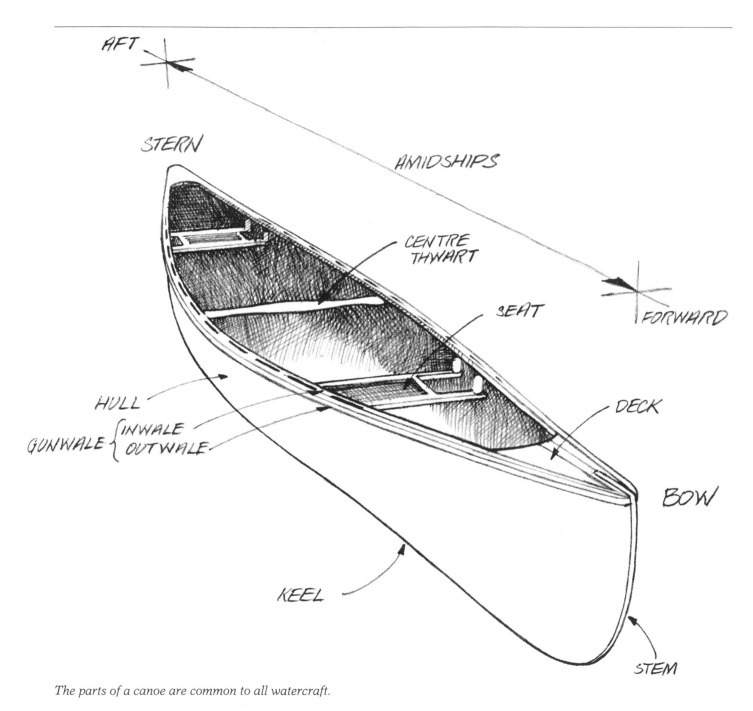

AFT

STERN

AMIDSHIPS

CENTRE THWART

SEAT

FORWARD

HULL

GUNWALE { INWALE / OUTWALE

DECK

BOW

KEEL

STEM

The parts of a canoe are common to all watercraft.

line (the curve of the hull or bottom edge), the shape of its bow and stern and its waterline length (hull length that is wetted when the canoe is in the water).

The *body plan* (on page 24) shows a canoe from the end, as if it were sliced crosswise at regular intervals, or stations, the shape and dimensions of which are each represented by a single line. Each cross section shows the accurate width and depth of the canoe at that point, as well as the shape of the hull bottom and the shape of the sides. A centreline drawn perpendicular to the waterline splits the cross section in two, but since each half is identical, only one half is shown in the body plan.

The *plan view* (on page 25) shows a fish's perspective of the canoe from directly underneath the boat, as if it were sliced end to end at regular waterlines. Each lengthwise section shows the true length and width at that level, as well as the contour from its maximum width to the point at each end. This describes the path the water must take at various levels as it moves from the entry line at the bow to the exit line at the stern. When the slices are superimposed over a common centreline, the plan view also indicates if the canoe is symmetrical (bow and stern halves are the same shape) or asymmetrical.

The Elements of Performance

Each of the many physical elements illustrated by the three

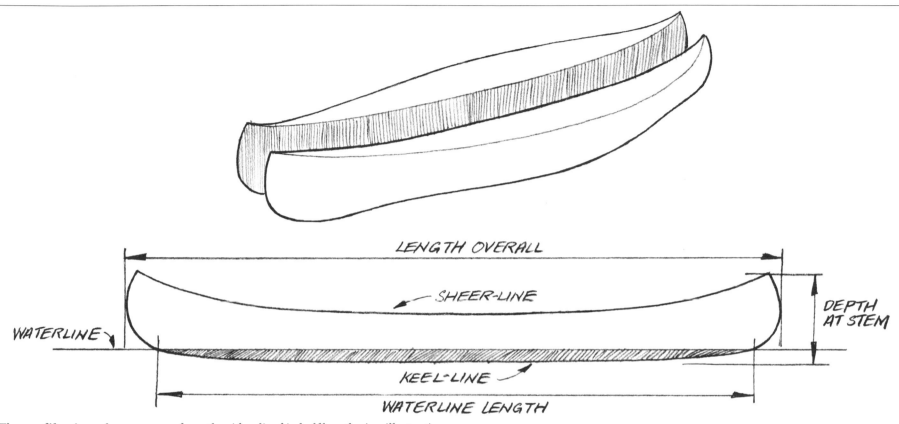

LENGTH OVERALL

SHEER-LINE

WATERLINE

DEPTH AT STEM

KEEL-LINE

WATERLINE LENGTH

*The **profile view** shows a canoe from the side, sliced in half lengthwise, illustrating the curve of the top and bottom limits as well as the length and depth of the canoe.*

views has a profound effect on a canoe's performance. Although they are discussed separately below, none of them acts in isolation. Each affects the others to some extent; in a well-designed canoe, they function in delicate balance.

Length

On average, the centre half of a well-designed hull provides 75 percent of its stability and carrying capacity, while the end quarters function primarily to part the wa-ters at the bow and bring them back together at the stern. Obvi-ously, a longer hull will carry more weight, but length also affects speed. Generally, the greater the waterline length and the higher the ratio of length to width, the faster the canoe and the easier it is to pad-dle. This is due partly to the phys-ics of waves and partly to the fact that in comparison to a short, wide hull, a long, narrow hull rides higher, with less wetted surface, and thus generates less friction against the water. A long hull will also track (hold its course) better than a short one but will not turn as easily.

Beam

This is the maximum width of a canoe. With a narrow beam, less effort is required to push the water aside and less friction is created by the hull surface. But, although a wide canoe generally paddles slower than a narrow one, it has greater carrying capacity and is more stable when loaded to its design capacity. Beam may be the same throughout the depth of the hull, in which case its sides are *plumb* (page 26). But if the maxi-mum beam occurs at the gunwales, the hull is *flared*. Most often found on narrow hulls, flared sides afford good "final stability." The hull be-comes more stable when it is loaded down because it becomes wider the lower it sits in the water. Flared sides also deflect waves.

When the gunwale beam is nar-

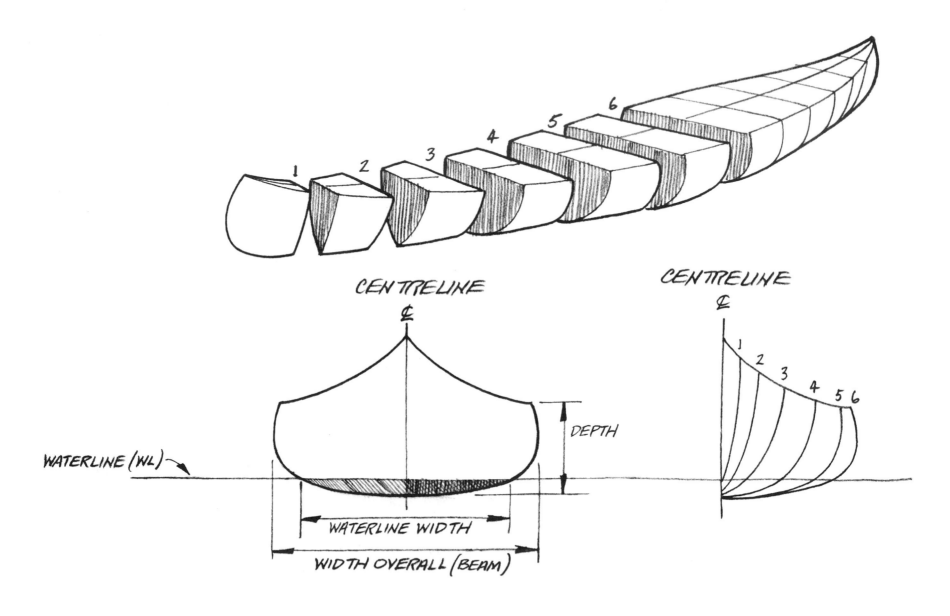

CENTRELINE

₵

CENTRELINE

₵

DEPTH

WATERLINE (WL)

WATERLINE WIDTH

WIDTH OVERALL (BEAM)

*The **body plan** is an end view of the canoe and shows it sliced crosswise at regular intervals, bow to stern, with the contours superimposed in sequence over a common centreline. It illustrates the depth and width of the canoe.*

rower than the maximum beam, the sides are *tumblehome* (they "tumble home"). Tumblehome is usually found on wider hulls, because the reduced gunwale width allows the paddler to reach over the side easily without sacrificing good carrying capacity. The arcing sides also help stiffen the hull. Although tumblehome does not affect initial stability, it can result in very poor final stability when too extreme and especially in combination with a wide, flat bottom.

Depth

The depth of a canoe is measured amidships from the gunwales to the bottom of the hull. This can range from 10 inches in a little solo canoe to more than 24 inches in a freighter. Depth is also measured at the bow and stern, from the top of the stem to the lowest point of the keel-line. *Freeboard*, another measurement of depth, is the distance from the water to the gunwales. When "capacity" is listed in canoe specifications, it usually refers to the weight that can be loaded into the canoe while retaining six inches of freeboard. But freeboard also affects the seaworthiness of a canoe. High sides will make it susceptible to wind, reducing speed and controllability, whereas low sides will render it susceptible to swamping in whitewater and waves.

Hull Contour

More important than depth, beam or length alone is the way

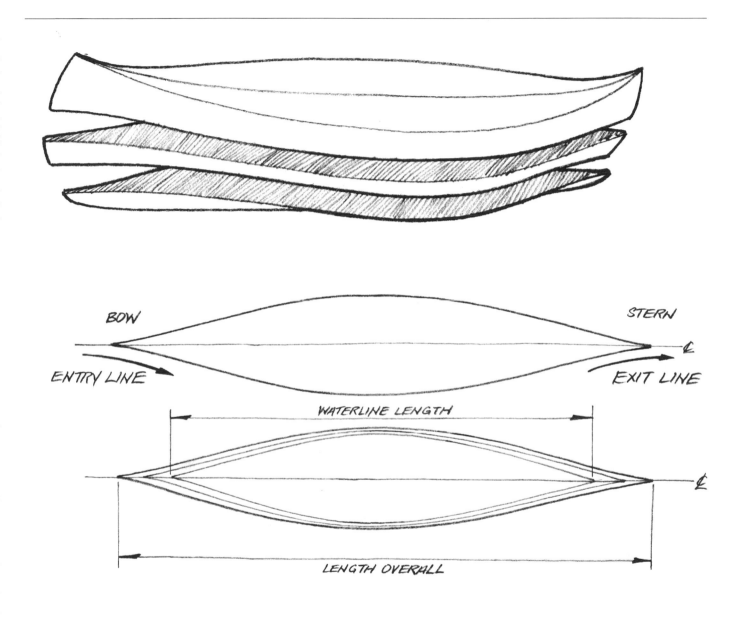

The **plan view** *is an underwater look at the hull sliced lengthwise at regular waterlines. It illustrates the shape of the hull bottom and the width and length of the canoe.*

these measurements are drawn together to form the hull contour. How this shape moves through the water is the key to canoe performance. A canoe has a displacement hull. It is basically a moving trough, dividing water at the bow and replacing it at the stern. Its efficiency depends on the amount of friction created by the hull surface meeting the water and the smoothness with which the water is displaced around its form.

A semicircular, or *round-bottom*, hull produces the least-wetted surface, but its tippiness makes it practical only for flatwater racing shells. A *flat-bottom* hull has the greatest wetted surface and is capable of carrying large loads. It can also turn quickly in every direction, making it appropriate for whitewater, where high manoeuvrability is a priority. This skidding action, however, means tracking can be difficult in anything less than glassy waters, and even then, flat-bottom hulls are slowed by high friction. Since it is buoyant over a large surface, a flat-bottom hull feels the most stable when you first climb in but only remains so in calm water. In rough water, the flat, buoyant hull follows the profile of the waves and can turn turtle suddenly when tipped past the sharp turn of its bilge. A flat bottom may be justified in freight canoes but is unsafe in recreational craft on anything but flat water.

The *shallow-arch*, or semi-elliptical, hull contour is a good compromise between the round and flat

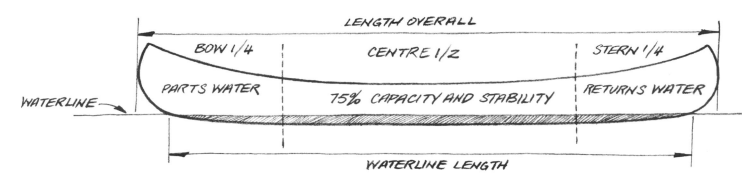

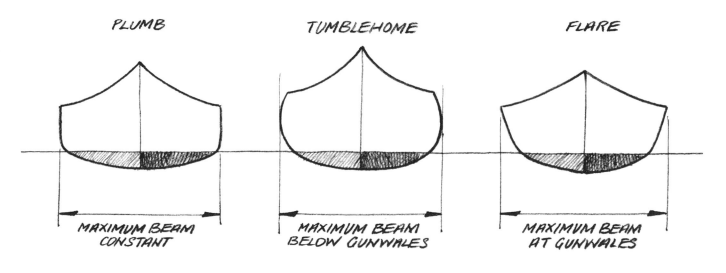

Top: *Up to half the length of a well-designed canoe is devoted primarily to parting the water at the bow and returning it at the stern. The longer the canoe, the faster it is.* **Bottom:** *The placement of maximum beam on the side of the hull determines the shape of the sides and the canoe's stability, speed and carrying capacity.*

bottoms. Its domed shape helps stiffen the hull, which is especially important with lightweight construction techniques, and reduces instability in the bilge area. Also, waves tend to slide under the boat. This hull feels "canoey," with good initial and final stability. Because such hulls take less abuse from heavy waters, naval architects often characterize them as "sea kindly." A shallow-arch hull will also track better than a flat hull. Because of its seaworthiness and average tracking and turning ability, this contour is the starting point for most general-purpose touring or cruising canoes.

A *shallow-vee* contour takes the hulls deeper and sharper into the water and produces slightly more wetted surface. Like the shallow-arch hull, the shallow-vee affords a high degree of final stability. But it tracks better, since the vee-shape functions like a keel, keeping the canoe on course. It is less responsive in turning, however. Because the shallow-vee cuts cleanly through waves, with little pounding or skidding, it is especially appropriate for sailing and lake canoes.

As a general rule, most hulls employ a combination of these forms. For instance, a cruiser might have a deep-vee bow to part the waters efficiently, opening gradually to a shallow-vee, then a shallow-arch to pass the waves cleanly along the hull, then narrowing back into a deep-vee at the stern. Such a design would com-

bine seaworthiness and directional stability with good manoeuvrability. It would also offer *reserve buoyancy* — extra width at the vee sections when the canoe sits deeper in the water.

Separate *keels* are the subject of some controversy in canoe design. They do add a measure of stiffness and protection to the hull bottom and will be much appreciated when paddling through a cross-wind on a lake, but that same keel will be roundly cursed when you try to manoeuvre through rock-strewn rapids. As a general rule, a shoe keel (a keel generally ⅜ by 2 to 3 inches wide) is a good idea for protection on a river boat, while a deeper keel is appropriate on a lake canoe, where manoeuvrability is less important than tracking ability. Keels should be avoided on whitewater canoes since they get hung up on obstructions and inhibit the sideways movement critical to dodging through rapids.

The *keel-line* of a canoe also affects manoeuvrability and directional stability. A straight keel-line from stem to stem will produce a fast, easy-paddling canoe that tracks exceedingly well but turns poorly. A keel-line that curves upward from the middle toward each end of the canoe is said to have *rocker*. Essentially, rocker lets the canoe pivot on its midpoint. The more rocker on the keel-line, the shorter the canoe's waterline length and the easier it turns and rises over waves. Too much rocker forces the centre of the canoe to

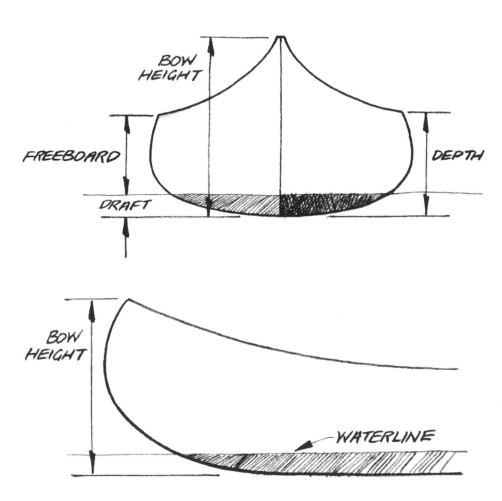

Determining the depth of the canoe: Freeboard, the distance between the gunwale and water, varies with the load the canoe is carrying.

support most of its weight, driving it deeper into the water, increasing displacement and friction and decreasing speed. Rocker can range from moderate lift in a cruiser to the banana-like profile of a competition slalom canoe. Poorly made or old canoes sometimes develop reverse rocker, or *hogged* keel-lines, which greatly inhibits performance.

Rather than a fully rockered keel-line, a canoe can have a slight *uplift* just at the stems. In a loaded boat, this allows enough of the hull to ride in the water for good tracking, but with the bow and stern riding slightly above the waterline, manoeuvrability and reserve buoyancy are improved.

The profile of the bow affects performance as well as the line of the hull body. Some bows rise vertically or on a slight incline, yielding a fairly straight sheer-line and maximum waterline length. This inclined or *plumb bow* forces the sides of the canoe to flare. The greater the incline, the more the sides must flare. Most traditional canoe bows, however, rise up out of the water and curve back slightly toward the paddler. This *recurve*, a logical extension of the rockered keel-line, reduces the area exposed to the wind for a given waterline length. But as the bow curves, it puts tumblehome into the sides, reducing reserve buoyancy. To compensate for this, extra height is often added at the stems. Extreme recurve, with a sharply rising sheer-line, makes

the canoe more susceptible to wind and adds some unnecessary weight, but the trade-off may be worth the beautiful sweeping lines thus achieved.

The *entry line* of a canoe — the shape of the forward point of the bow that cuts the water — plays a large part in its efficiency. The smoothness with which water is displaced around the hull affects both speed and the amount of effort required to attain it. A canoe that carries its fullness well into the ends must quickly push aside a large volume of water, which tends to slow down as it moves along the hull. Thus the canoe tends to plow through the water. On the other hand, a hull with a fine entry line moves the water aside more slowly. Because the displaced fluid has more time to get out of the way, the paddler exerts less of his own force to move it. The fine lines part the water neatly, producing little spray and a small set of waves that accelerate naturally along the hull. Fine entry lines are desirable under all conditions, albeit in varying degrees. A flatwater cruiser should have the finest entry, whereas a whitewater canoe must have its fullness carried as far forward as possible, without disturbing the fine entry.

Although traditional canoes are generally symmetrical in shape, some modern designers have abandoned that principle. In an *asymmetrical* design, the beam is placed slightly aft of centre, creating a longer bow. Paddling and tracking

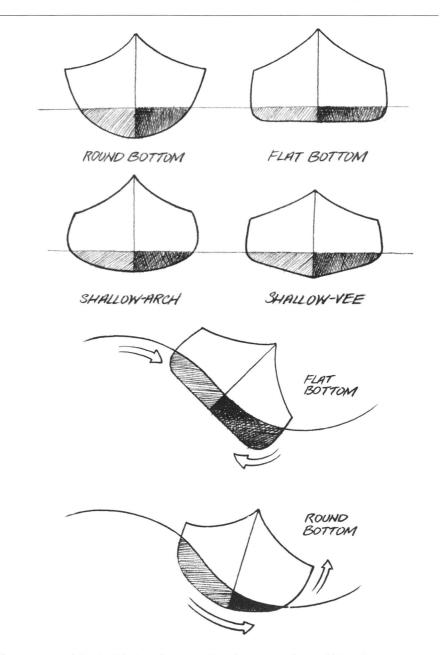

The contour of the hull below the waterline determines how efficiently a canoe cuts through water. Rough waves slide harmlessly under a shallow-arch hull, because the deeper it sits, the wider and more stable the hull becomes.

become easier because of the fine entry of the long bow and the extra buoyancy in the stern quarter.

Compromises and Conundrums

Between the blunt-nosed, flat-bottomed freighter and the stiletto racer, there are infinite variations in canoe design. But at the same time, there is no ideal form. Each of the principles discussed above can be manipulated for specific results, but the gain of one advantage inevitably entails the loss of another. If you opt for tracking, you will sacrifice manoeuvrability, while the extreme rocker that offers optimal manoeuvrability will rob your canoe of tracking ability. Even within each design variable, there are no absolutes. Final stability is a prime concern if you are out for a paddle with the kids, but it is a low priority if you delight in the solo canoe "ballet" of Bill Mason. And finally, however functional a well-designed canoe may be, it must also be visually pleasing, balancing practicality with beauty of line. The flexibility of canoe design, however, is its own reward. All these disparate elements can be orchestrated in several different ways to produce a variety of canoe prototypes well suited to different requirements. If there is no such thing as the perfect all-purpose canoe, there are several types available that do specific jobs very well.

A *cruising*, light-tripping or general-purpose canoe should have a

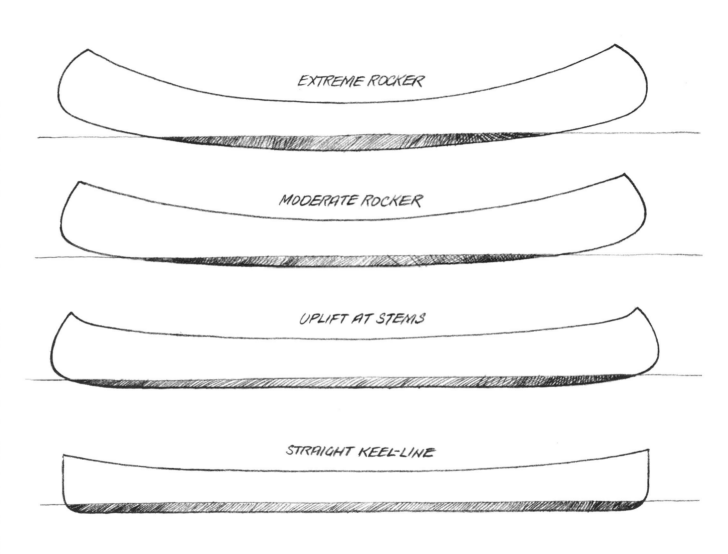

EXTREME ROCKER

MODERATE ROCKER

UPLIFT AT STEMS

STRAIGHT KEEL-LINE

Even without a keel, the profile of a hull bottom strongly affects paddling performance and the way the canoe rides out rough waters. Keel-lines range from the razor's edge of a racing cruiser to the extreme rocker of a slalom canoe. Most recreational canoes fall somewhere between the extremes.

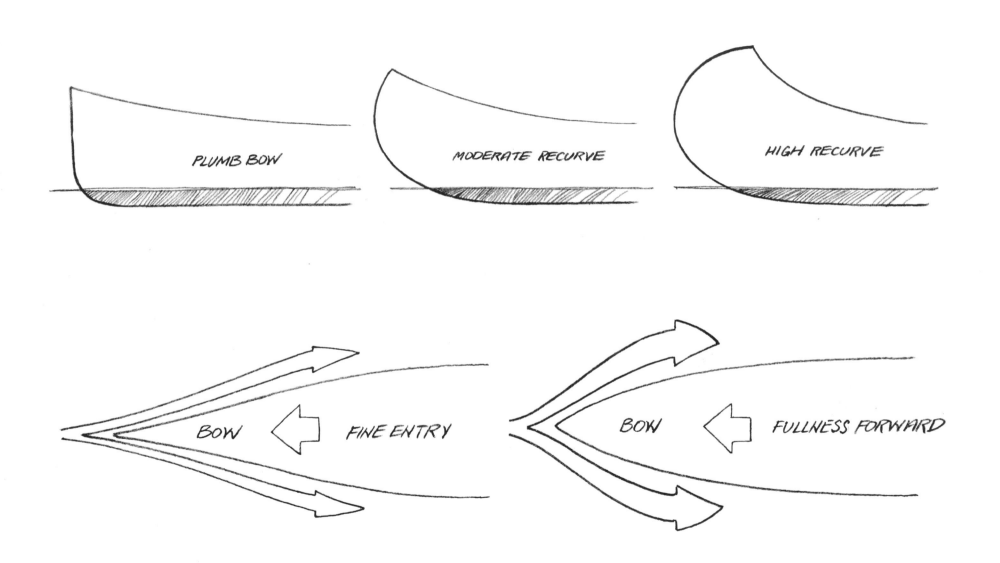

Above: *A plumb bow forces the sides of a canoe to flare, while traditional recurved bows result in tumblehome sides. High recurve is traditionally attractive but can make the canoe susceptible to wind.* **Below:** *Fine entry lines part the waves more smoothly than a blunt-nosed bow that plows the water. The result is greater speed with less paddling effort.*

keel or vee end-sections, a fairly straight keel-line and a fine entry line for good tracking and efficient paddling. The hull should be shallow-arch or shallow-vee with low stem profiles. Asymmetrical designs are appropriate. Overall length can range between 14 and 18.5 feet, with at least a 12-inch depth and beam between 30 and 34 inches.

A *wilderness*, or tripping, canoe must be suited to all the conditions of extended bush travel – large lakes, shallow streams, whitewater and portages – while retaining the ability to carry sufficient gear. The hull should be as full as possible toward the bow and stern without disturbing the fine entry, with a slight uplift or rockered keel-line for manoeuvrability in rough water and a shallow-arch contour. A bit of tumblehome in the sides is ideal. The hull should be keelless or shoe-keeled, and weight is a definite consideration. Competent wilderness canoes are at least 16 feet and as much as 18.5 feet long, with a 12- to 14-inch depth and 34- to 36-inch beam.

A *whitewater* or *downriver* canoe should have a shallow-arch to flat-bottom hull, well rockered for easy turning and with a good lift at the ends so it can ride through heavy rapids without taking water. Moving the bow seat back somewhat will improve this ability. Keels are undesirable, unless a shoe-keel is considered necessary for protection. In any case, a whitewater canoe has to be strong enough to

The Bettmann Archive Inc

withstand inevitable encounters with rocks. Decks should be long and gunwales wide enough to shed water, with tumblehome sides to accommodate the beam. The consideration of weight has to be balanced against durability. Dimensions are similar to those for a wilderness canoe, although depth should be about 14 inches.

The design of a *solo* canoe depends on the individual canoeist's paddling technique. A traditional Canadian-style solo canoe, paddled heeled over, is 14 to 15 feet, with a symmetrical shallow-arch hull. Widths range between 25 and

34 inches, with a slight tumblehome to the sides. The traditional American Rushton-style solo canoe, on the other hand, is paddled flat with a double blade. It is typically narrower (24 to 30 inches) and shorter (10 to 14 feet), with a shallow-arch/shallow-vee hull. The paddler sits on the hull bottom, supported by a back rest. The contemporary Gault-style solo canoe, a new design now fashionable in the United States, is paddled well heeled over. It is also narrow (24 to 30 inches), with shallow, flared sides and an asymmetrical hull 13 to 16 feet long, with a

rounded-vee bottom and soft bilges.

After digesting this chapter, you may not be ready for the world of custom design, but you should be able to set your own personal performance priorities. As one builder exclaimed after mastering the mysteries of canoe design: "I'm not trained, but now I certainly can tell an ugly canoe when I see one, and I have a pretty good idea about how poorly it must handle." In the next chapter, you will find plans for seven canoes that are as sweet in the water as they are on the shelf.

PIPE DREAMS TO PAPER

Choosing the Right Plan

The one great principle, far too often forgotten — that a comfortable boat, like a shoe or a coat, must be built for the wearer and not worn down to his shape.

— *John MacGregor*

"There is no more perfection in canoes than in wives," Professor Edwin Fowler of the Knickerbocker Canoe Club of New York City observed in 1883. "There are only convenient compromises.

"An ideal canoe is a bundle of compromises, yielding something of her paddling speed to be able to sail fairly, sacrificing a portion of her sailing lines to secure reasonable lightness and sharpness, losing somewhat of her steadying weight and momentum for the sake of portability, and being less portable because she must be strong and stiff. . . .

"A canoe must be equally at home with wings for the breezes and with paddles for the water, yet be able to move on the legs of her master over dry land."

With all due respect to Professor Fowler, the perfect canoe (and no doubt the perfect wife) does exist. There are hundreds, even thousands of them – a perfect canoe for each discriminating paddler. Unfortunately, though, what is perfect for one canoeist is not necessarily right for another, as everyone has his own tastes and needs.

On the following pages are the plans for seven canoes that reflect some of the most desirable shapes in canoes. They range in size from the sleek 20-foot C-4 racer to the shapely 15-foot Hiawatha, from the beamy whitewater Prospector to the vee-bottomed English cruiser, from the sporty Dean Sunnyside to the ultimate cottager's ca-noe, the Peterborough.

Armed with the plan of your choice, you can readily build a beautiful and functional canoe in a matter of weeks. The plan, though, as many novices are surprised to discover, does not really show how to build a canoe at all; rather, it gives the dimensions and lines of a mould upon which your canoe can be built. Once the mould is built exactly to specifications, you use it as the foundation for a shell of ¼-inch-thick wooden strips that are glued together to form the hull.

While early canoe moulds were solid replicas of hulls, our mould consists only of a series of plywood forms cut to resemble several exact cross sections of the canoe. Each of these forms is called a "station," and they represent the width, height and shape of the hull of a classic canoe carefully measured at 12-inch intervals.

Mounted on a straight and simple wooden platform called the strongback, the station moulds become the canoe's skeleton, and you have only to add its woodstrip skin.

Of course, your own design priorities may differ from this book's plans, and you may want to check the Sources (page 143) for other plans or turn to the end of this chapter to discover how to modify an existing plan by adding a little extra length here or a bit of rocker there to produce your own perfect canoe.

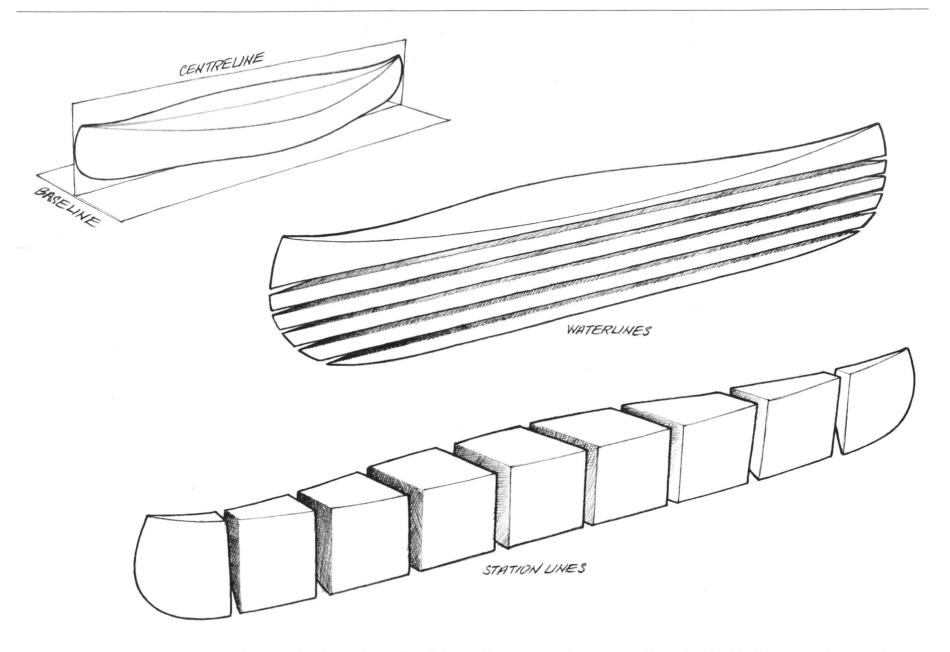

CENTRELINE

BASELINE

WATERLINES

STATION LINES

This page (top to bottom): *Canoe in relation to its baseline and centreline; divided by various waterlines; and segmented at its stations.* **Opposite page:** *Chart A shows a station's contours measured up from the baseline to the hull bottom, while Chart B measures out from the centreline to the side of the hull — plotted together, they show the full curve of the hull at that point. Nails and a batten are used to draw the points' curve.*

READING PLANS

Before beginning the construction process, you must learn to read the basic plans (found on pages 40 through 53). While confusing at first, you will realize that they simply show three different views of the same canoe: a side view, a bottom view and a head-on view. And they all have two reference lines in common: the *baseline*, a horizontal bow-to-stern plane upon which the hypothetical canoe sits, and the *centreline*, which runs from bow to stern (perpendicular to the baseline) and divides the canoe in half neatly down the centre. Because each of the three views have both these reference lines in common, you can pick any point of the canoe at random, and by relating its position to the baseline and the centreline on one perspective, you can readily find that exact same point on the other two views. This enables you to create a three-dimension mould of the canoe.

While the plan and profile perspectives are straightforward enough, the body plan tends to cause confusion. In this chapter, we have offered six designs for symmetrical canoes that have identical front and back halves, and one asymmetrical canoe whose bow and stern sections have different dimensions.

Turn to page 41, and examine the body plan at the centre of the page. Now imagine that you are looking at a canoe head-on. The first thing you will notice is that the left side of the hull is missing. That is because the left side is a mirror image of the right and can be reproduced by simply flopping the view over. The second thing you should notice is that there are numbered lines curving out different distances from the centreline. Each of these lines represents one station of the canoe and shows the exact shape of the canoe hull at that specific spot. As previously mentioned, the stations are measured at 12-inch intervals, starting at the midpoint of the hull and ending 1 foot from the bow. So if you build a full-sized mould of each station shape (complete with a matching left-hand side) and attach them to a strongback in correct sequence and properly spaced, you will have a perfect skeletal replica of the front half of the canoe. By producing an extra copy of each station mould, you will be able to add the rear half of the canoe mould to the strongback at the same time, if the canoe is symmetrical. If the canoe is asymmetrical, the body plan has a second series of lines on the other side of the centreline to show the shape of the hull's back half.

Opposite the line drawings on the plan is a sketch of the finished model, a short description of its background and performance capabilities and a list of specifications. There is also a chart called the Modified Table of Offsets, which is the indispensable link between the plans and the actual canoe you choose to build. While

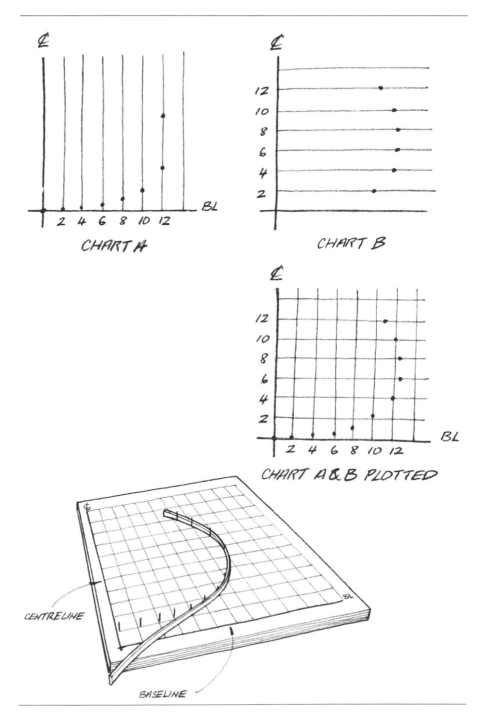

CHART A

CHART B

CHART A & B PLOTTED

CENTRELINE

BASELINE

the body plan shows you the contours of the canoe from a head-on perspective, it would be difficult to produce the station moulds from this scaled-down model, so to ease the process, a Table of Offsets is used. The figures in the table arithmetically trace the contours of the hull at each station, indicating where the outside edge of the hull falls in relation to the centreline and the baseline. By plotting each of the points given in the table onto full-size graph paper and joining them in a smooth curve, you can reproduce the exact inside shape of the hull's bottom and sides. Transferred onto plywood, your full-scale body plan becomes the mould for a station. Complete directions for drawing out the plans follow.

The Modified Table of Offsets found in this book is a simplification of the standard offsets that are traditionally used to scale up all three views of a canoe. While standard offsets give the builder enough information to construct station moulds, the intervals between stations are usually 24 inches instead of our 12, too far apart for the woodstrip/resin technique. Thus while you may find plans through various sources for other interesting canoes, they will not necessarily have tables of offsets suitable for woodstrip/resin construction, and you will have to adapt them. Adapting such plans requires lofting — drawing all three views of the boat, full size, on the floor of the boatshop "loft" — then measuring out stations at 12-inch intervals. Lofting is an involved procedure, the subject of entire books (see Sources, page 143). But it is the key to design freedom, and to quote yacht designer Bud McIntosh, "Any damn fool can learn it in two hours."

For those who find a suitable canoe among the plans at the end of this chapter, lofting will be unnecessary, but if it is, read them with a caveat borrowed from legendary canoebuilder J. Henry Rushton:

"It will be impossible — even if it were desirable — to have any one model, any one mode of construction or any one builder please all. It depends very much upon the individual canoeist, as well as the waters upon which he will use his canoe, as to what model will suit him best."

DRAWING THE PLANS

Tools:

  square
  straight edge
  pencil
  batten
  ruler

Materials:

  tracing paper
  finishing nails
  masking tape

To draw out the full-scale plans, first prepare the graph paper. Tape a large, square sheet of tracing paper firmly to a piece of plywood. Mark off a grid of 2-inch squares as

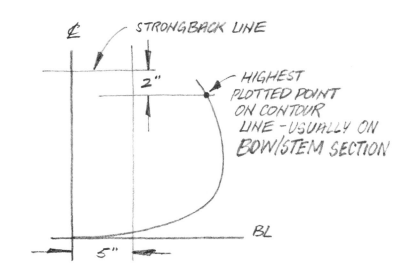

Establishing the strongback line

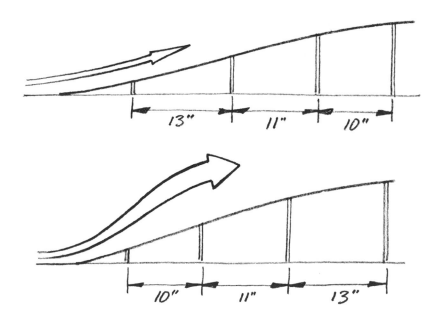

By altering the distances between stations, the shape of the canoe can be changed significantly, affecting the way it cuts through water.

accurately as possible, designating the lowest horizontal line as the baseline and the vertical line on the far left as the centreline. All stations and the stem will be drawn, one at a time, on this single plan sheet to keep things simple and to save paper.

To plot the points of intersection for Station #1, refer to Chart A of the Modified Table of Offsets. At the baseline, mark where the first station meets the centreline. Moving along the baseline, mark where that station intersects each vertical line. Note that Chart A details the bottom contour of the station.

Turn to Chart B and plot the rest of the points for Station #1. By starting at the baseline and proceeding up the centreline at 2-inch intervals, you will find the contour of the side of the hull. Together, they delineate one half of the first station of your canoe mould.

After plotting all the points for one station, tap 1-inch finishing nails at enough of the points to produce a fair curve. Bend a flexible batten (1/8 x 3/8 x 36-inch pine or plastic strip) smoothly along the nails, and with a sharp pencil, draw a line connecting the points.

Continue drawing each mould contour in the same way until the tracing paper looks like a full-size replica of the body plan.

Although the outside contour of each mould has been drawn, it lacks an upper limit to complete the form. On your graph, draw a full-length vertical line 5 inches to the right of (and parallel to) the

centreline. Connect the highest plotted point to this line with a horizontal line, and continue vertically up 2 inches and, finally, back horizontally to the centreline. This top horizontal line is the *strong-back line* and indicates where the station mould will join the strong-back when you construct your mould skeleton. Finish off each contour on your plan by connecting the highest point of each station horizontally to the 5-inch line, then continue up vertically to the common strongback line.

DESIGNING YOUR OWN

Canoes have been around almost as long as the human race; there has been ample opportunity for design innovation. Thus there is really no such thing as a new canoe, only recombinations and adaptations of the lines of old ones. If you can find a plan that meets most of your criteria, it is fairly simple to adjust some of the design variables like length, rocker and entry line. Unless you have had considerable paddling experience, however, it is better to build a professional design than to risk disaster on launching day.

Should you decide to design your own, start by finding a plan with the basic hull shape that you want, and cut out the moulds according to the directions on page 82. It is then relatively simple to vary the canoe length by manipulating the distance between stations. Master builders like Rushton often used one mould for two or

CLAMP FEET TO LEGS

The jig to take lines off a canoe should have long, adjustable legs that can be quickly dismantled to transfer the hull's contours to paper.

three different lengths of canoes. Ideally, stations should be spaced 12 inches apart, but that interval can be stretched to 14 inches without sacrificing the essential quality of the shape. Over a total of 15 stations, this adjustment will extend a design by more than 2 feet. Conversely, a design can be shortened by shrinking the distance between stations, or if you have a symmetrical design that is both too long and too beamy, you can produce a shorter, slimmer canoe by omitting the centre mould but setting up the remaining stations as specified.

When the stations remain equidistant, most basic design characteristics of the canoe stay the same despite the changed length. But

because the waterline length and length-width ratios are changed, speed and ease of paddling may be affected. When the distance between stations is varied unequally, the curve of the waterline is changed fundamentally. For a longer entry line, the stations can be moved progressively farther apart toward the bow. For increased fullness in the front quarter, the stations can be moved progressively closer together toward the bow.

You can also alter the shape of the keel-line by modifying the height of the moulds. A flat keel-line can be equipped with a 1-inch rocker, first by raising the centre mould 1 inch, then tacking a batten along the centreline from stem to stem and raising the other moulds to its level. The practice of clamping temporary battens along the hull at regular intervals to check for fairness and to avoid surprises during planking is recommended for any of these modifications. More complex modifications can only be done by lofting the plans first. It will save you time and energy in the long run.

TAKING OFF LINES

It may happen that the canoe you want to build is already in the water — with someone else in the sternman's seat. This is how I started, not with a set of plans but with a canoe upturned on my bed. Using a ruler and paper cutouts, I made patterns that fit inside the canoe. After tracing these onto boards and painstakingly cutting out the moulds, I realized that my mould had reproduced every hump and hollow, every warp and twist of the model canoe I had copied.

Other authors may claim that taking lines off an existing boat can be that simple, but in fact, there are no shortcuts. You do not want a replica of that exact canoe — you want to reproduce its lines as drawn by the original designer. That can only be done by taking off the lines at 24-inch centres, lofting the canoe, then taking the measurements at 12-inch centres. By using centres of 18 to 24 inches (I recommend 10 to 14 inches), builders are not giving enough support

to their ¼-inch strips and will experience a nightmare of twists and humps as they lay up the canoe.

One can learn lofting from other boatbuilding manuals, but I have developed what I find to be a simple and accurate way of taking the lines off. Set the hull upside down on sawhorses, so that it is perfectly level. (It will help considerably to start with a level floor.) Run a strip of masking tape down the centreline of the canoe and find the midpoint between the stems. Starting here, measure toward each end, marking the tape at 24-inch centres. If the canoe is symmetrical, only mark one half.

Clamp a thin piece of wood to each stem, extending above the hull. Stretch a taut line between them, parallel to the centreline, and ½ to 1 inch above the highest point on the canoe. This is the baseline, the horizontal point of reference.

On a piece of heavy paper, draw a baseline at the top and a centreline down the middle. Draw waterlines at 2-inch intervals parallel to the baseline. At the midpoint of the canoe, measure the width across the gunwales, and plot it on the plan paper. Measure the distance from the top of the hull to the taut line (baseline), and mark this point on the plan.

Make a jig as illustrated and set it over the hull, clearing the taut line. (A level on top will ensure that the jig is sitting square.) Staple scraps of planking to the jig at frequent intervals so that their tips

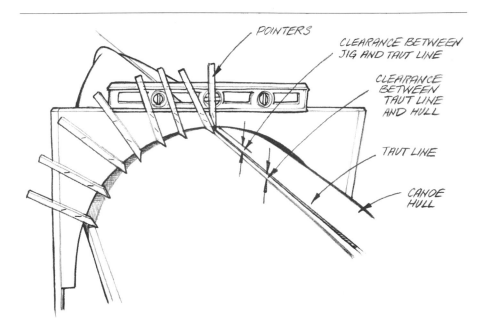

With the levelled jig at a station, staple scraps of planking at frequent intervals so that their points show the curve of the hull.

rest against the hull, indicating the curve of the hull from centreline to gunwales. One pointer should mark where the taut baseline lies in relation to the actual canoe contours.

When all the pointers are in place, lay the jig on the paper, matching the taut line point with the baseline/centreline intersection and the gunwale points with the premeasured width. Mark all the points indicated by the pointers, and draw them into a fair curve with a batten.

Continue in the same manner at each station. At the stems, measure from the wooden upright to the hull at regular intervals, and plot the points of the stem curve.

When the body plan is finished, measure along the waterlines from the centreline to the contour to make up a Table of Offsets. Using the Table of Offsets, go through the lofting process, then take off the lines at 12-inch intervals. Remember to deduct the projected thickness of the hull from the lofted drawings.

However you have procured them — by lofting, buying or drawing one of the models in this chapter — you now have the full-size contours of your canoe hull on a single sheet of paper. Before you can translate that into a boat, you need to assemble your materials and tools, and clear yourself a space you can call a boatshop.

THE PLANS

The following seven designs were chosen to span the most desirable and beautiful shapes in canoes. Each plan includes perspective line drawings, a Modified Table of Offsets and construction specifications as well as a short description of the background and primary functions of that particular model.

PETERBOROUGH 40
CHESTNUT PROSPECTOR 42
ENGLISH 20 44
HIAWATHA 46
C-4 48
REDBIRD 50
SUNNYSIDE CRUISER 52

Peterborough

A "Peterborough" often referred to any open Canadian-style canoe, but this design comes from the company that made the town's name famous around the world. A direct descendant of the first "white man's canoe" created by John Stephenson 125 years ago, it is one of the main models built in the original cedarstrip technique. Its narrow beam and shallow arch hull make it ideal for general purpose paddling and light tripping. Keeled, with a slightly rockered keel-line, it is responsive and easy to paddle. This favourite of the lake district has justifiably been dubbed "the cottager's canoe."

CHART A

Measured up from baseline and out from centreline at 2" intervals.

+ = + 1/32"
− = − 1/32"

Distance from centreline	STATION NUMBERS								BOW/STERN SECTION
	0	1	2	3	4	5	6	7	
Centreline 0"	1 3/16 + "	1¼ + "	1 3/8"	1 7/16"	1 5/8"	1 7/8"	2 5/16"	3 3/16"	1¾"
2	1 3/16 +	1¼ +	1 3/8	1 7/16 +	1 11/16 +	2 9/16	3 13/16	7 3/16	1 13/16
4	1¼ +	1 5/16 +	1 3/8 +	1½ +	2 1/8	3 7/16	6 1/8		1 7/8 +
6	1 3/8	1 7/16	1½	1 11/16	2¾ +	4 13/16	10 13/16		2 1/16 +
8	1 9/16 +	1 5/8 +	1¾ +	3 15/16	7¾ +				2 5/16
10	1 15/16	2	2 5/16 +	3 3/8 +	6 1/8				2 5/8
12	2½	2¾	3½	5 9/16					3
14	3 11/16	4 1/8	6 3/8 +						3½ +
16									4 3/8
18									5 5/8
20									7 9/16
22									11 1/16 / 18 3/8
SHEER	13½	13 9/16	13 11/16	13 13/16 +	14 1/8	14 13/16	16 1/16	18¾	

CHART B

Measured out from centreline and up from baseline at 2" intervals.

+ = + 1/32"
− = − 1/32"

Distance up from baseline	STATION NUMBERS								BOW/STERN SECTION Measured out from Station #6
	0	1	2	3	4	5	6	7	
2"	10 7/16"	9 15/16"	9"	7 3/8"	3 5/8"	7/16"			5 3/16"
4	14 5/16	13 7/8	12 9/16	10 11/16	8 1/8	5	2¼ "	½"	15 5/16
6	15 3/8	14 15/16 +	13 7/8 −	12¼	9 15/16	7	3 15/16	1½ +	18 7/16 +
8	15 5/8	15¼ +	14 5/16 −	12 13/16	10¾	8 1/8 −	5 1/8	2¼	20 5/16
10	15 3/8	15 1/16	14 3/16 −	12 7/8	11 +	8 5/8 +	5 13/16	2¾	21½
12	15	14 11/16 +	13 13/16	12 9/16	10 15/16	8¾ −	6 1/16	2 15/16	22¼ +
14					10 5/8	8 9/16	6	3 −	22 9/16 +
16							5¾	2 7/8	22½
18								2 5/8 +	22 1/16 +
20									21 7/16 +

SPECIFICATIONS:

Length	15' 10¾"
Depth	12¼"
Maximum beam	31¾"
Gunwale beam	30"
Bow height	21"
Weight	50-58 lbs.

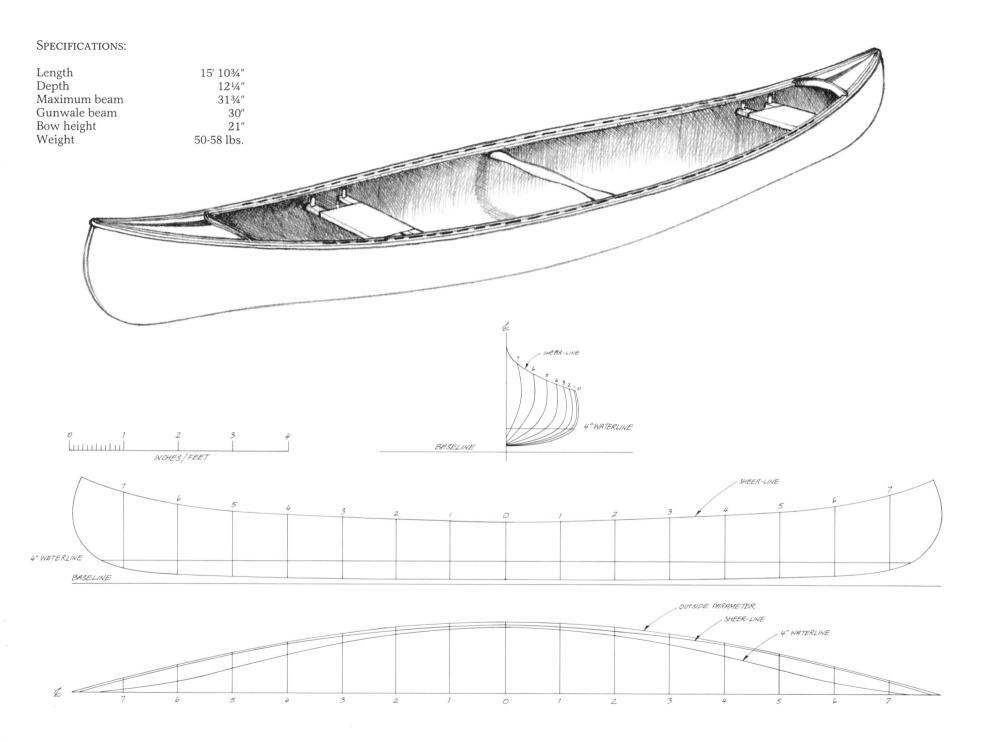

INCHES / FEET

C̵L̵
SHEER-LINE
7
6
5 4 3 2 1 0
4" WATERLINE
BASELINE

SHEER-LINE
7 6 5 4 3 2 1 0 1 2 3 4 5 6 7
4" WATERLINE
BASELINE

OUTSIDE PARAMETER
SHEER-LINE
4" WATERLINE
C̵L̵
7 6 5 4 3 2 1 0 1 2 3 4 5 6 7

SPECIFICATIONS:

Length	16′
Depth	14″
Maximum beam	35″
Gunwale beam	34″
Bow Height	25″
Weight	58-62 lbs.

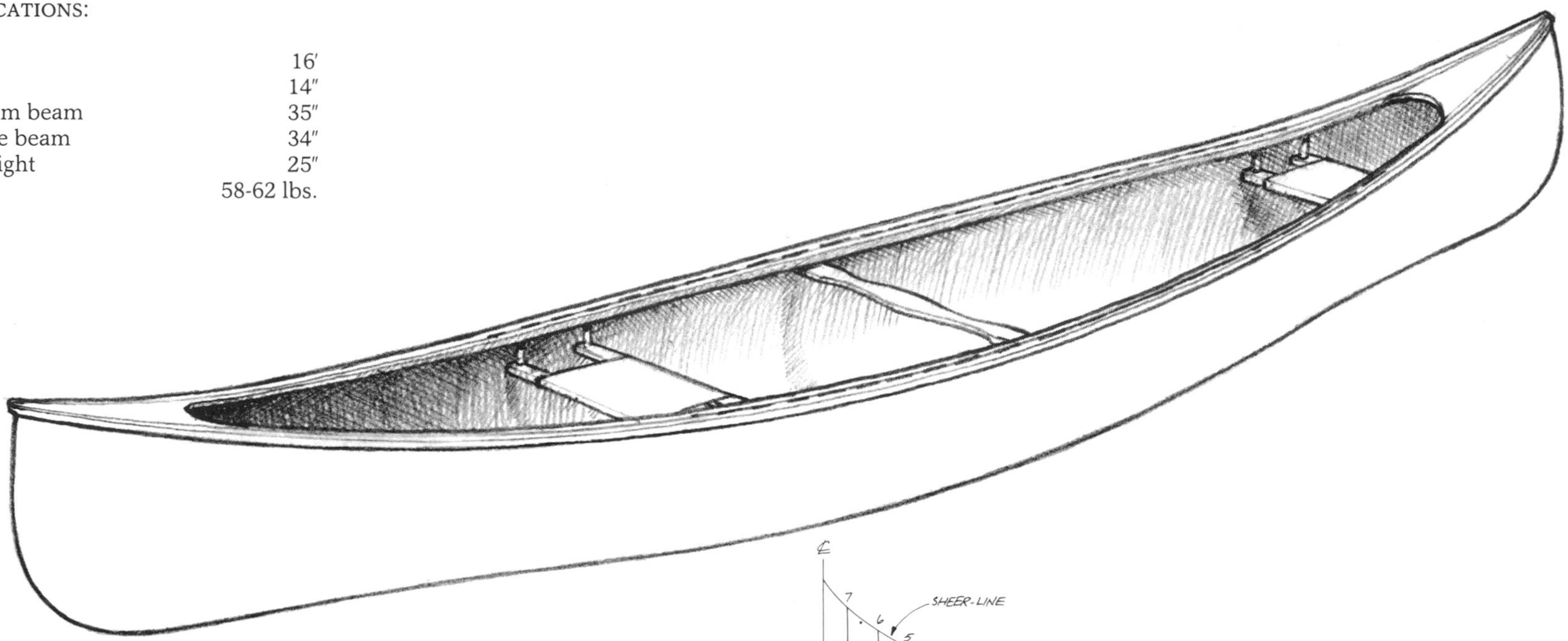

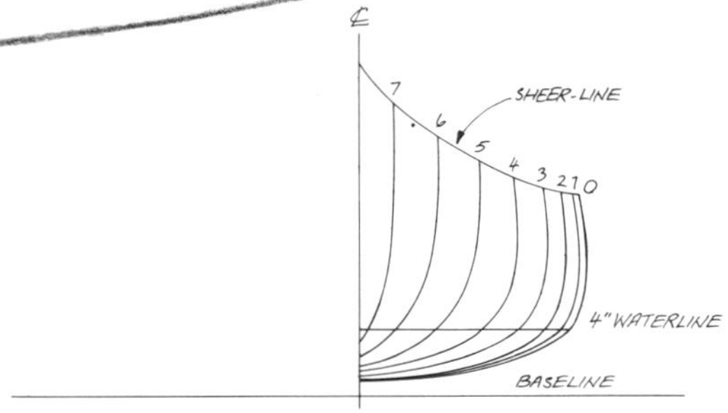

℄
SHEER-LINE
7 6 5 4 3 2 1 0
4″ WATERLINE
BASELINE

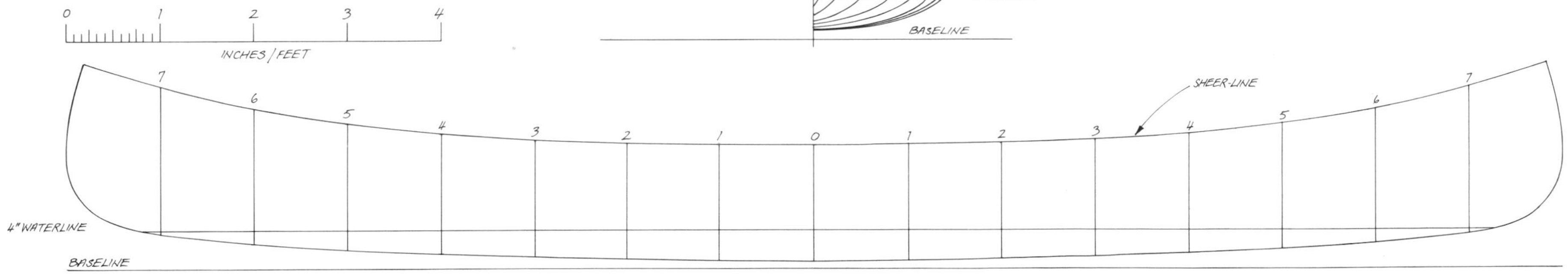

0 1 2 3 4
INCHES / FEET
7 6 5 4 3 2 1 0 1 2 3 4 5 6 7
SHEER-LINE
4″ WATERLINE
BASELINE

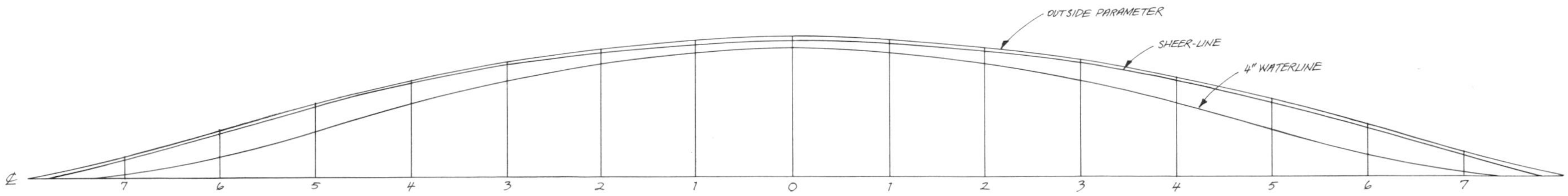

OUTSIDE PARAMETER
SHEER-LINE
4″ WATERLINE
℄
7 6 5 4 3 2 1 0 1 2 3 4 5 6 7

Chestnut Prospector

This "workhorse of the North" was designed in Canada to meet the specific needs of the prospector — good manoeuvrability through whitewater and wilderness, with capacity to carry substantial loads. The Prospector features a flattened, shallow arch hull with its fullness carried into the bow and stern, increased depth amidships to maintain freeboard, and deepened ends to keep paddlers and gear dry. The rockered keel-line makes it very manoeuvrable in whitewater. This is the favoured canoe of Bill Mason, Canada's premier paddler: "It is amazing that such a large-volume tripping canoe can also be so beautiful to paddle solo in the leaned position — canoe ballet, as I call it. It is the ideal all-round canoe."

CHART A

Measured up from baseline and out from centreline at 2" intervals.

+ = + 1/32"
− = − 1/32"

Distance from centreline	0	1	2	3	4	5	6	7	BOW/STERN SECTION
Centreline 0"	1/4"	5/16"	7/16 +"	3/4"	1 1/16	1 1/2 +"	2 1/4 +"	3 7/8 +"	2 13/16"
2	1/4 −	5/16 −	1/2	13/16	1 1/8 +	1 7/8 +	3 1/2	8 7/16	3
4	5/16	3/8 +	5/8	15/16	1 9/16	2 7/8 −	6 +		3 3/16 +
6	7/16 +	9/16	7/8	1 3/16	2 1/4	4 7/16			3 7/16
8	3/4	7/8 −	1 3/16 +	1 5/8 +	3 1/4	7 1/16			3 11/16
10	1 3/16	1 1/4	1 3/4	2 1/2	4 15/16				3 15/16
12	1 3/4	1 7/8	2 7/16 +	3 7/8 +					4 1/4
14	2 11/16	2 7/8	3 13/16	7 1/2					4 5/8
16	4 1/2	4 7/8							5 1/8 +
18									5 15/16
20									7 1/8
22									9 3/8 / 21 7/8
SHEER	14 3/4	15 +	15 5/16	15 5/8 +	16 5/16	17 1/2	19 1/2	22 1/4	

CHART B

Measured out from centreline and up from baseline at 2" intervals.

+ = + 1/32"
− = − 1/32"

Distance up from baseline	0	1	2	3	4	5	6	7	BOW/STERN SECTION Measured out from Station #6	
2"	12 5/8 −"	12 5/16"	10 7/8"	8 15/16 +"	5 5/16"	2 5/16"	0"			
4	15 5/8	15 3/8	14 3/16 −	12 1/16 +	9 1/16	5 9/16	2 1/2	1/16"	10 7/16"	
6	16 3/4	16 1/2	15 3/8	13 1/2	10 3/4 +	7 3/8	3 15/16 +	1 1/8	18 3/16	
8	17 1/8	16 7/8	15 13/16	14 1/8	11 9/16 +	8 3/8 +	4 7/8 +	1 7/8 +	20 15/16	
10	17 1/8 +	16 15/16	16 −	14 5/16 +	11 15/16	8 13/16	5 7/16	2 5/16	22 3/8	
12	17	16 13/16	15 15/16	14 5/16 +	12	9 −	5 11/16 +	2 9/16 +	23 +	
14	16 7/8	16 11/16	15 13/16 +	14 1/4	12 −	9 +	5 13/16 +	2 3/4	23 3/16 +	
16					11 7/8	9 1/16 +	5 13/16	2 3/4 −	23 1/8	
18							5 13/16 −	2 11/16	22 13/16	
20								2 9/16	22 3/8 +	
22								2 7/16	21 15/16	
24									21 7/16	

English 20

According to Gilbert Gordon, William English "built just about the best canoe in Peterborough." Although not as well known as the Peterborough and Lakefield Canoe Companies, English was a respected builder. His original mould for this design, still in use today, testifies to the efficiency and beauty of English lines. Designed for regattas, the #20 is a vee-bottom racing canoe that compromises capacity for speed. According to Walter Walker, who continues to build the English #20 in the original cedarstrip technique, "It is not just a pleasure canoe for the average man, but anybody who is a good paddler likes it."

CHART A

Measured up from baseline and out from centreline at 2" intervals.

+ = +1/32"
− = −1/32"

Distance from Centreline	STATION NUMBERS									BOW/STERN SECTION
	0	1	2	3	4	5	6	7	8	
Centreline 0"	¾"	11/16"	7/8"	1 1/16"	1 5/16"	1 5/8	2 1/8"	3¼ –"		1 9/16
2	7/8	15/16	1 1/16	1 5/16+	1 15/16	2 11/16	4¼ +	8 3/8+		1 7/8
4	15/16+	1 1/16	1¼ +	1 5/8	2 11/16	3 7/8	7+			2¾ +
6	1 1/8	1¼ –	1½ +	2	3½	5 7/8+				2 15/16
8	1 5/16+	1 7/16+	1¾ +	2 9/16	4 7/16+	8 1/16+				3 1/16
10	1¾	1 7/8	2 3/8+	3½	6 1/16					3¼
12	2 5/16+	2 7/16+	3 5/16+	5 1/8+						3 7/16
14	3 9/16+	3 13/16	5½							3 7/8
16										4½
18										5 5/8
20										7¼
SHEER	12 5/8	12 5/8	12¾ +	13 1/8+	13¾ +	14 11/16	15¾	17½		

CHART B

Measured out from centreline and up from baseline at 2" intervals.

+ = +1/32"
− = −1/32"

Distance up from baseline	STATION NUMBERS									BOW/STERN SECTION Measured out from Station #6
	0	1	2	3	4	5	6	7	8	
2"										
4	14 3/8"	14 1/8+"	12 7/8"	10¾ +"	7 1/8"	4 3/16+"	1¾ +"	3/8 –"		14 7/16"
6	15 3/16+	15	14¼	12 9/16+	9 15/16	6 9/16	3 3/8	1 3/16+		18½
8	15 5/16	15 3/16	14½ +	13¼	11 1/8	7 15/16	4 9/16	1 7/8		20 5/8
10	15 3/16	15	14 3/16	13 5/16	11½	8 11/16	5 7/16	2 7/16		21 7/8+
12	14 7/8	14¾	14 1/16+	13 1/16+	11 3/8+	8 15/16+	5 15/16	2¾ +		22 7/16+
14					11 1/8	8 13/16+	6 1/16	3		22 7/8+
16							6	3 1/16+		22 15/16
18								3 1/8		22 11/16
20										22 5/16

SPECIFICATIONS:

Length	16'
Depth	12"
Maximum beam	31"
Gunwale beam	30"
Bow height	21¼"
Weight	52-56 lbs.

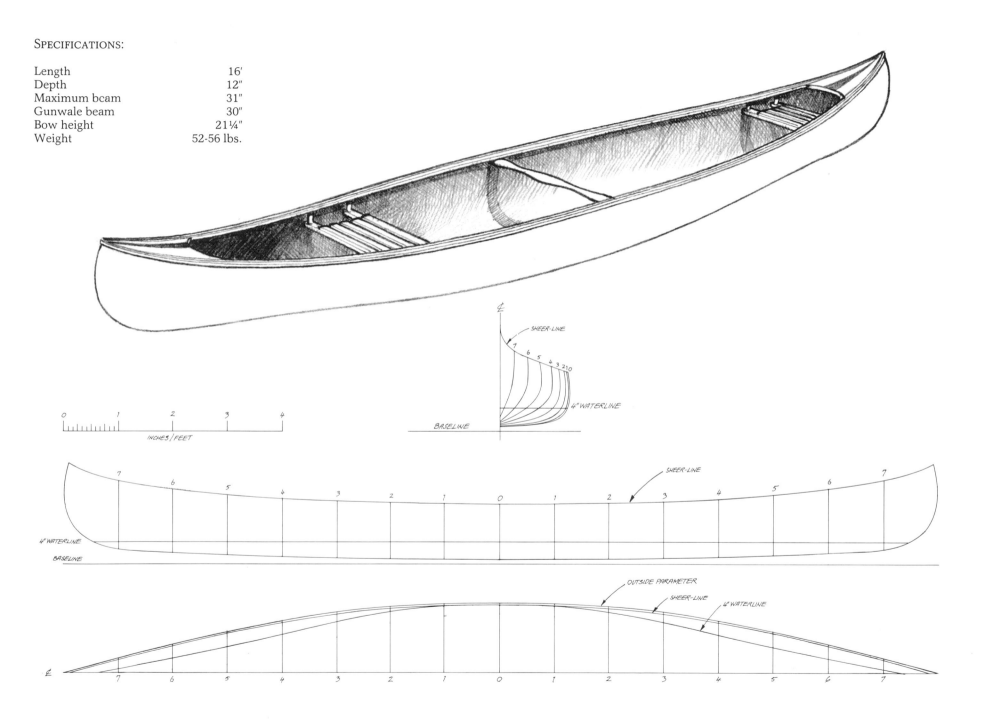

SHEER-LINE

4" WATERLINE

BASELINE

0   1   2   3   4

INCHES/FEET

7   6   5   4   3   2   1   0   1   2   3   4   5   6   7

SHEER-LINE

4" WATERLINE

BASELINE

OUTSIDE PARAMETER

SHEER-LINE

4" WATERLINE

7   6   5   4   3   2   1   0   1   2   3   4   5   6   7

Specifications:

Length	15'
Depth	12¼"
Maximum beam	33"
Gunwale beam	33"
Bow height	21"
Weight	48-50 lbs.

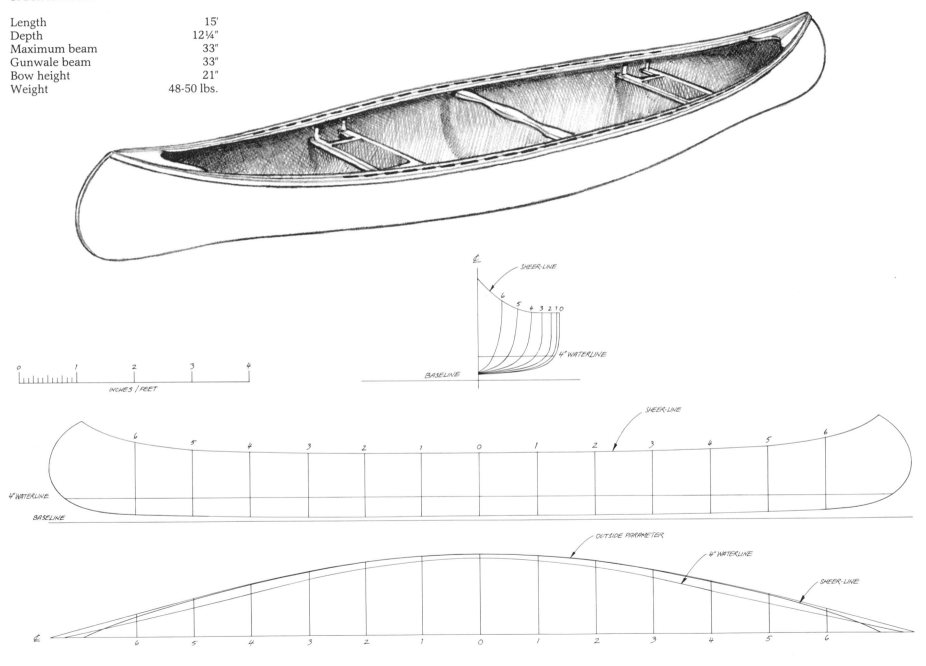

SHEER-LINE

6 5 4 3 2 1 0

4" WATERLINE

BASELINE

0   1   2   3   4

INCHES / FEET

SHEER-LINE

6   5   4   3   2   1   0   1   2   3   4   5   6

4" WATERLINE

BASELINE

OUTSIDE PARAMETER

4" WATERLINE

SHEER-LINE

6   5   4   3   2   1   0   1   2   3   4   5   6

Hiawatha

This Bear Mountain design* has a look that is as traditional as its name, its sheer-line and bow profile harking back to the native forebears of modern canoes. Its underbody, however, has been shaped to conform to the most up-to-date concepts in paddling efficiency. The hull is a shallow arch with a moderately flat keel-line that flows into a shallow vee to become a fine deep vee at the bow for directional stability, speed and manoeuvrability. The vee is carried as far back as possible so that it acts like a keel for tracking. As a general purpose or light tripping canoe, it was designed in the tradition of contemporary American cruisers, achieving its optimum waterline shape when paddled level, not heeled over.

*Copyrighted design; permission required for commercial reproduction.

CHART A

Measured up from baseline and out from centreline at 2'' intervals.

+ = +1/32''
− = −1/32''

Distance from centreline	0	1	2	3	STATION NUMBERS 4	5	6	7	8	BOW/STERN SECTION
Centreline 0''	1¼''	1¼''	1¼+''	15/16+''	1 3/8+''	1 5/8''	1 15/16''			2 3/8+''
2	1 3/8−	1 3/8	1½+	1 11/16	1 7/8	2 5/8	4¼+			2½−
4	1½	1 5/8−	1 7/8−	2 1/8+	2 5/8−	4 1/8				2½+
6	1¾−	1 7/8−	2¼	2¾−	3¾	7 7/16				2 9/16
8	2	2¼−	2 5/8	3 7/16	5 11/16	8 3/8				2 11/16+
10	2½−	2 11/16	3¼	4 11/16+						3 1/16
12	2 7/8+	3 3/8	4 3/8	8¾						3¾
14	4 3/16	4½	7¼+							4 15/16 / 19 5/16
16	6 13/16									7 3/16 / 16 7/16
SHEER	13 3/16	13 3/16	13 3/16	13 3/16	13½	14 5/16	16 1/8			

CHART B

Measured out from centreline and up from baseline at 2'' intervals.

+ = +1/32''
− = −1/32''

Distance up from baseline	0	1	2	3	STATION NUMBERS 4	5	6	7	8	BOW/STERN SECTION Measured out from Station #6
2''										
4	13¾''	13¼''	11½''	9 1/16''	6 3/8''	3 7/8''	1 13/16''			12 9/16''
6	15 11/16	15 1/16	13 7/16	11+	8 3/16	5 3/8	2 7/8			15 1/8
8	16¼	15 5/8	14 1/8	11 7/8	9 1/8	6 1/8	3 5/16+			16 7/16
10	16 5/16+	15¾	14 5/16	12 1/8	9 7/16	6½	3 5/8			17 1/16
12	16 5/16+	15 13/16	14 3/8	12 3/16+	9 5/8	6 5/8+	3¾+			17¼
14						6 11/16+	3¾			16 15/16
16							3 5/8			16 3/16
18										15 1/16−
20										13 7/16

C-4

C-4 canoes are not cruisers; they are used for flat-water racing, in a straight line, on a measured course. The original C-4 was built by Walter Dean in the early 1900s, and is owned by the Mississauga Canoe Club. This revised model was designed for the Mississauga Club, based on the lines of the Walter Dean original. Ted has since modified the shape, taking out all rocker and filling out the stern a little above the waterline to increase reserve buoyancy when the boat is paddled fast. Long and narrow, this canoe is built for speed with a deep vee hull, flared sides and plumb bow to produce the maximum waterline length. An excellent club project for experienced builders! (N.B. No stem mould dimensions are given so that builders can design a bow and stern suitable to their own purpose.)

CHART A

Measured up from the baseline and out from the centreline at 2" centres.

+ = + 1/32''
− = − 1/32''

Distances from centreline	STATION NUMBERS																		
	1	2	3	4	5	6	7	8	9	10	11	12	13	14	15	16	17	18	19
Centreline 0"	1 9/16 +"	1 3/8 +"	1 3/8"	1¼ +"	1¼ +"	1¼ +"	1¼ +"	1¼ +"	1¼ +"	1¼ +"	1¼ +"	1¼ +"	1¼ +"	1¼ +"	1¼ +"	1¼ +"	1¼ +"	1 3/8"	1 7/16"
2	7 1/8	3 7/8	2 15/16	2 7/16	2 1/8+	1 15/16+	1 15/16	1¾	1¾	1 11/16+	1 11/16	1¾	1 13/16	1 7/8	2	2¼ +	2 5/8	3 7/16	7 3/8
4		7½ +	4 13/16+	3 11/16+	3 3/16	2¾ +	2 9/16	2 3/8	2¼	2 3/16	2 3/16	2¼ +	2 3/8+	2¼ +	2 15/16	3 7/16	4 3/8	7 1/8 +	
6		13½ +	7 7/16+	5 3/8	5 3/8	3 11/16+	3 5/16+	3 1/16	2 13/16+	2¾	2 13/16	2 7/8+	3 1/8	3 7/16+	4 1/8	5 1/8	7 9/16		
8			11 7/8	7 13/16+	6+	4 15/16+	4¼ +	3 7/8+	3 5/8+	3½	3 9/16	3¾	4 1/8+	4 13/16	5 15/16	8 1/8+	14¼ +		
10			11 15/16	8 3/8	6 11/16+	5 11/16	5 1/8+	4¾ +	4 9/16	4¾	5 1/16	5 13/16+	7 1/16	9 3/16	14 9/16				
12						12 9/16	9 9/16	7 15/16+	7 1/16+	6 5/8+	6 3/8	6 11/16	7 3/8	8 7/8+	11 9/16				
14							12 5/16	10 5/8	9 15/16+	10	10 13/16+	12 3/16+							

CHART B

Measured out from centreline and up from baseline at 2" intervals.

+ = + 1/32''
− = − 1/32''

Distances up from baseline	STATION NUMBERS																		
	1	2	3	4	5	6	7	8	9	10	11	12	13	14	15	16	17	18	19
2"	11/16''	1 3/8 +''	2 3/16''	3 1/16''	3 7/8 +''	7 11/16 +''	5 7/16''	6 3/16''	6¾ +''	7''	6 13/16 +''	6½''	5 7/8''	5 3/16 +''	7¼ +''	3 7/16''	2 9/16''	1 11/16 +''	7/8''
4	1 7/16''	2¾ +	4¼	5 11/16	6 15/16+	8 1/8	9 3/16+	9 7/8	10 3/8	10 11/16	10 7/16	10 1/16	9¼	8 5/16	7 3/16	5 15/16+	7 9/16+	3 1/8	1½ +
6	2+	3 7/8	5¾ +	7½ +	9 1/16	10 5/16+	11 3/8+	12+	12 3/8	12 9/16+	12 5/16	11 7/8	11	10 1/16	8 7/8+	7 7/16+	5 13/16	4	1 15/16 +
8	2 7/16	4 9/16+	6 7/8	8 11/16+	10 7/16	11 11/16+	12 11/16	13 3/16	13 9/16	13 5/8+	13 3/8	12 7/8+	12 1/16	11 1/8+	9 15/16+	8 7/16	6 5/8+	4½ +	2 5/16
10	2¾ +	5¼	7 11/16	9 5/8+	11 3/8+	12 11/16+	13 9/16	14 1/8+	14 3/8+	14 3/8	17 1/16+	13 5/8+	12¾ +	11 7/8	10 11/16	9 1/8	7 3/16+	5+	2 9/16
12	3 1/16	5 13/16+	8 5/16+	10 5/16+	12 1/16+	13 3/8	14 3/16	14¾	14 15/16	14 7/8	14 9/16	14 3/16+	13 5/16	12 3/8	11 1/8+	9 11/16+	7 11/16+	5 7/16+	2¾ +
14	3¼	6 3/8	8 13/16+	10 7/8+	12 9/16	13¾	14 9/16+	15 1/16+	15¼ +	15 3/16	14 15/16+	14 11/16	13¾	12¾ +	11½ +	10 1/8+	8 3/16+	5 7/8+	3+

SPECIFICATIONS:

Length	20'
Depth	14"
Maximum beam	30"
Gunwale beam	30"
Bow height	14"
Weight	70 lb. min.

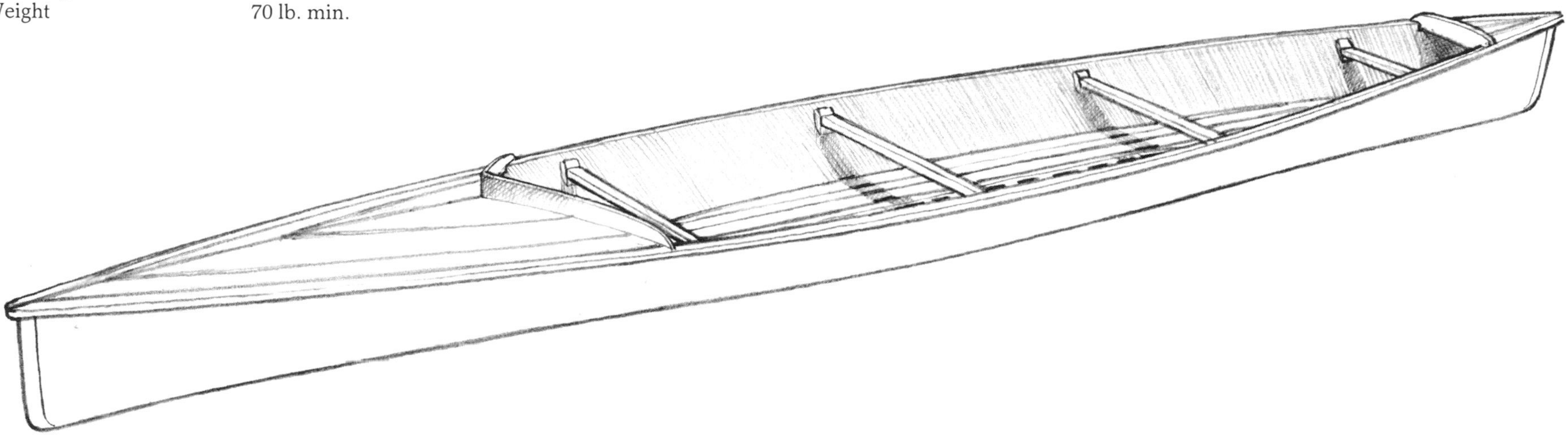

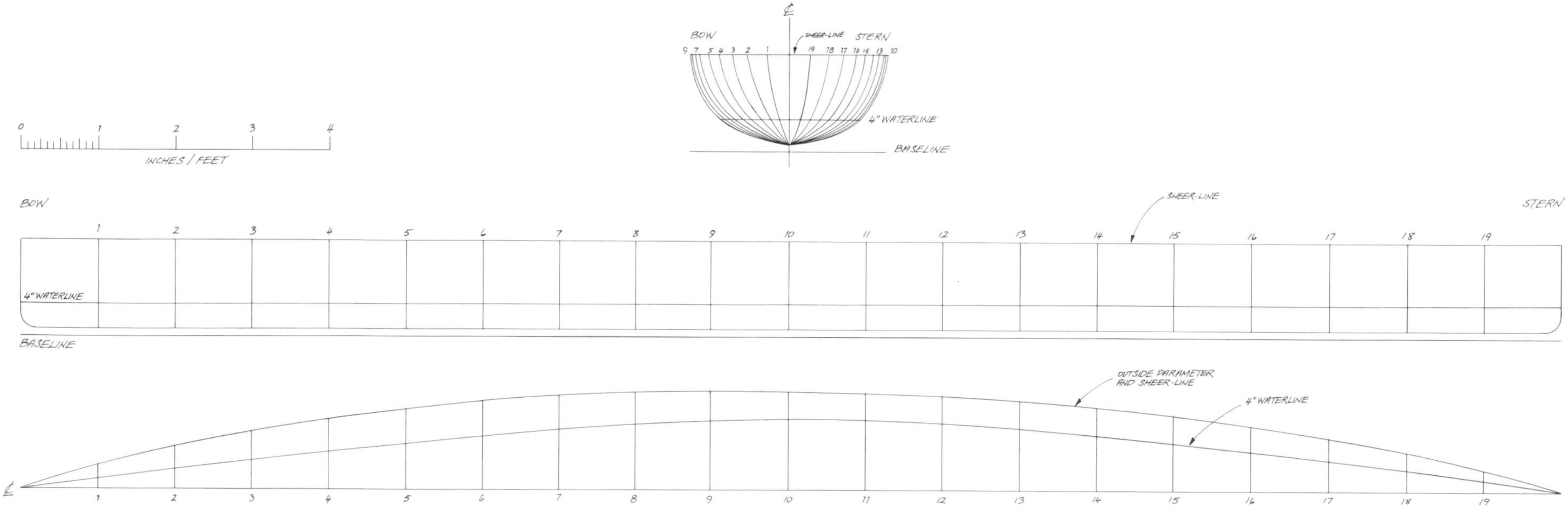

BOW

CL

SHEER-LINE   STERN

9 7 5 4 3 2 1   19 18 17 16 15 13 10

4" WATERLINE

BASELINE

0   1   2   3   4

INCHES / FEET

BOW   SHEER-LINE   STERN

1   2   3   4   5   6   7   8   9   10   11   12   13   14   15   16   17   18   19

4" WATERLINE

BASELINE

OUTSIDE PARAMETER
AND SHEER-LINE

4" WATERLINE

1   2   3   4   5   6   7   8   9   10   11   12   13   14   15   16   17   18   19

SPECIFICATIONS:

Length	17'6"
Depth	12"
Maximum beam	33½"
4" waterline beam	31"
Bow height	21"
Weight	52-56 lbs.

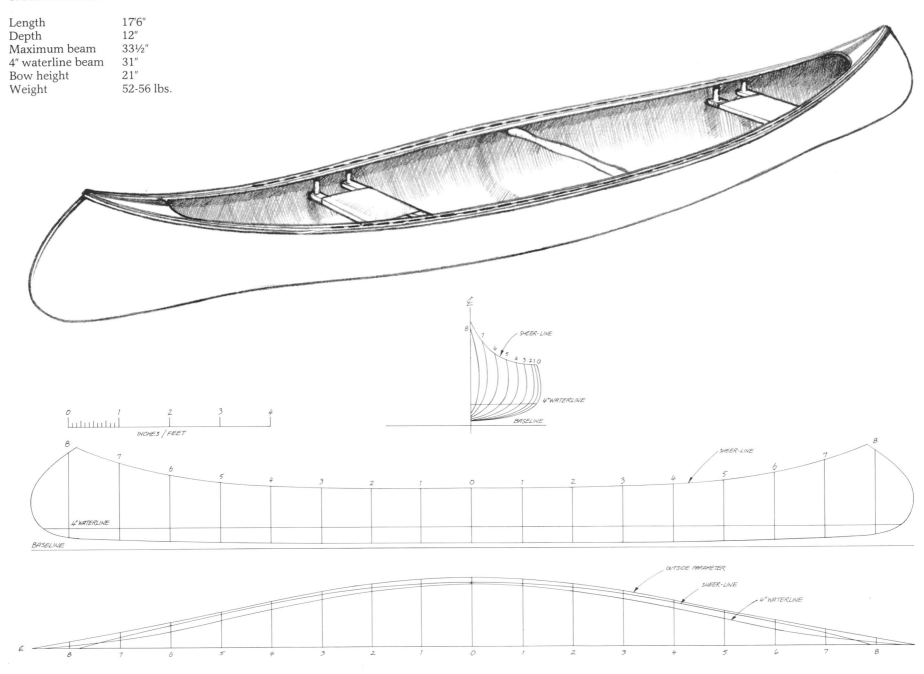

INCHES / FEET

SHEER-LINE

4" WATERLINE

BASELINE

4" WATERLINE

BASELINE

OUTSIDE PARAMETER

SHEER-LINE

4" WATERLINE

Redbird

This Bear Mountain design* is an efficient wilderness canoe that has proved exceptionally seaworthy, even in the heavy seas around the Magdalen Islands in the Gulf of St. Lawrence. Its keelless shallow-arch hull with moderate rocker combines with a long waterline and fine entry to make it a fast responsive boat. The bow and stern profile are reminiscent of the Long Nose Ojibwa Rice Harvesting canoe. The sides are moderate tumblehome for improved lateral strength and allow outwales wide enough to turn aside waves and spray. As one delighted builder reported, this boat is "very sweet in the water — an excellent touring and tripping canoe."

CHART A

Measured up from baseline and out from centreline at 2'' centres.

+ = +1/32''
− = −1/32''

Distance from centreline	0	1	2	3	4	5	6	7	8	BOW/STERN SECTION
Centreline 0''	1¼''	1 5/16''	1 3/8''	1 7/16''	1 9/16''	1¾''	2''	2 7/16''	3 7/16+ / 21¼''	2 15/16''
2	1 5/16	1 3/8	1 7/16	1 5/8	1 7/8	2 5/16+	3	4 5/16		3
4	1 7/16	1½+	1 5/8+	1 7/8+	2 3/8	3 1/8	4 5/16	8/14¼		3 1/8+
6	1 5/8+	1 11/16+	2+	2 5/16+	3+	4 3/16	7			3 3/16−
8	2	2 1/16+	2½	3+	4 1/16	6 5/16				3¼
10	2 7/16	2 9/16	3 1/8+	4	5 7/8+					3 7/16
12	3 1/8	3 3/8	4 1/8	5 11/16						3¾−
14	4 1/8	4 9/16+	5 15/16							4 3/16− / 20 3/8
16	6½ / 11 15/16									4 15/16 / 18 13/16+
18										6 3/16+ / 16 13/16
SHEER	13	13 1/16	13¼	13½	13 7/8	14 3/8+	15 3/8	17 13/16	21¼	

CHART B

Measured out from centreline and up from baseline at 2'' intervals.

+ = +1/32''
− = −1/32''

Distance up from baseline	0	1	2	3	4	5	6	7	8	BOW/STERN SECTION Measured out from Station #7
2''	8''	7 11/16''	5 15/16+''	4 9/16''	2 9/16''	1''				
4	13¾+	13 3/16	11 13/16−	10	7 15/16	5¾	3 5/8''	1¾''	5/16''	13 3/8''
6	15 13/16−	15¼+	14+	12 3/16+	10 1/16	7¾+	5 7/16	3 3/16	1 1/8+	17 11/16+
8	16 3/8−	15 7/8	14¾	13 1/16	11	8¾+	6 7/16	4 1/16	1 5/8+	19 7/16+
10	16 5/16	15 7/8	14 7/8−	13¼	11¼+	9 1/16	6¾+	4 5/16	1 7/8−	20 1/8+
12	16−	15 5/8	14 9/16+	13 1/8	11 3/16−	9−	6¾	4 5/16	1 13/16	20 3/16
14						8¾+	6 3/8+	4 1/16	1 5/8+	19 11/16−
16								3 9/16	1 3/8	18 5/8−
18									15/16+	16 7/8
20									3/8+	14 9/16

Sunnyside Cruiser

Developed by Walter Dean in 1910 for use in the Lake Ontario waters off Sunnyside Beach, Toronto, this fast, efficient cruiser often doubled as a "girling" canoe. It was so popular that it soon accounted for 90 percent of Dean's business. Narrow, with plumb sides and a shallow vee hull, it cuts through flatwater neatly. Graceful yet jaunty, it has the "Dean" elevated decks with a coaming to sweep aside spray. Advertised as "the handsomest canoe in the world," it is the ultimate in a luxurious, easy-paddling recreational canoe.

CHART A

Measured up from baseline and out from centreline at 2" intervals.

+ = +1/32"
− = −1/32"

Distance from centreline	STATION NUMBERS 0	1	2	3	4	5	6	7	BOW/STERN SECTION
Centreline 0"	1½"	1½"	1 5/8 – "	1 5/8 + "	1¾"	1 15/16"	2 7/16"	2 11/16"	2 5/8 – "
2	1 5/8	1 11/16	1 13/16	1 7/8 +	2 1/8 +	2¾ +	4 ¼	7 1/16	2 5/8
4	1¾	1 7/8 –	2	2 3/16	2 5/8 +	3 13/16	6½ +		2 5/8 +
6	2	2 1/8	2 3/8	2 5/8	3 3/8	5½			2¾ –
8	2 3/8	2 9/16	2 7/8	3 5/16	4 9/16	8¾			2¾
10	3 1/8	3 5/16	3¾	4½	7 1/16				2¾ +
12	4 5/16	4½ +	5 3/16	6 7/8 +					2 13/16
14	6 9/16	6 7/8 +	8 5/8 +						2 13/16 +
16									2 7/8
18									3
20									3 7/16 / 15 15/16
22									4 5/8 / 12 13/16
SHEER	13 5/8	13¾	13 7/8	14 1/16 +	14 3/8	14¾	15 3/16	15 5/8 +	

CHART B

Measured out from centreline and up from baseline at 2" intervals.

+ = +1/32"
− = −1/32"

Distance up from baseline	STATION NUMBERS 0	1	2	3	4	5	6	7	BOW/STERN SECTION Measured out from Station #6
2"									
4	11 9/16 + "	11¼"	10 7/16 + "	9 5/16"	7 3/16 + "	4¼"	1¾ + "	13/16"	21 5/16"
6	13 11/16	13 7/16 +	12¾	11 7/16 +	9 3/8	6 7/16	3 5/8	1½ +	22 15/16
8	14 9/16 +	14 7/16	13 13/16	12 7/16 +	10 3/8	7 11/16 +	4 7/8 +	2 3/8 –	23 1/16 +
10	15	14 13/16 +	14 3/16	12 7/8	10 7/8	8 5/16 +	5½ +	2¾	22 9/16
12	15 1/8	15	14 5/16	13	11 1/16	8 5/8	5¾ +	2¾ +	21 9/16 +
14				12 15/16	11	8 5/8	5¾ +	2 5/8	20 3/8
16									19

SPECIFICATIONS:

Length	16'
Depth	12⅜"
Maximum beam	30¾"
Gunwale beam	30¾"
Bow height	14¾"
Weight	48-54 lbs.

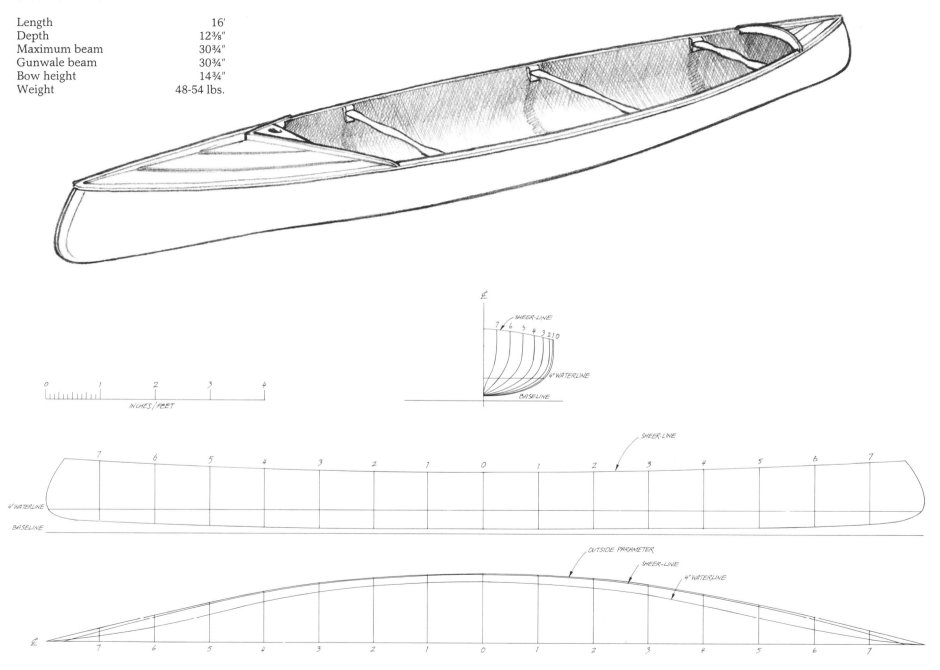

PREPARATIONS

Setting up the Workshop

The integrity of the boatbuilder is his most valuable asset.
— Bud McIntosh

Judging by the meticulous craftsmanship of a classic Otonabee cedarstrip, or a modern Bear Mountain canoe, one would think that each had emerged from an orderly shop equipped with the finest in precision tools. A glimpse into my dusty warren, however, is as reassuring as the fading photographs of Thomas Gordon's boatworks. Canoe builders, it seems, have always plied their trade in cramped and cluttered quarters — Gordon's canoes took shape in an abandoned church on a Lakefield back street; a dilapidated farm-implement outlet on the outskirts of Bancroft, hung with sliced cedar and ageing moulds, is home to Bear Mountain canoes. In the end, one comes to realize that a canoe can be built anywhere, with very little equipment — only the quality of materials can never be compromised.

WORKPLACE

A boatshop is ultimately wherever you make it. An empty hayloft may seem an appropriate, even romantic, workshop, set amidst curious spiders and darting swallows. But slanting shadows through the barnboard, dusty residues and shifting temperatures will probably prove it less than ideal.

In selecting your own boatshop, you should consider size, climate control and ventilation. While perfect conditions are desirable, you will undoubtedly have to make compromises. After all, it is better to put up with a second-class shop than to abandon your dream canoe.

Will It Fit?

The workshop need not be huge, but to be comfortable, there should be at least two to three feet, free and clear, around the whole canoe. At some stages, you may need a helper, and tripping over each other will not improve the mood or efficiency.

When sizing up a potential boatshop, remember that what came in as thin flexible pieces of wood must go out as a full-fledged canoe. This may seem like an old joke, but it happens. One Scarborough builder had to remove a window and two rows of bricks to get his canoe to water. He says he planned it that way. Do not surprise yourself with an unplanned renovation.

Aside from the strongback and emerging canoe, you will need room for a bench or work surface to hold tools, materials and mugs of coffee, a place to store strips where they will not get mangled and, if you are machining your own parts, an area long enough to rip lumber. Electrical outlets will be appreciated, and a level floor is a real bonus.

One essential piece of furniture cannot be overlooked — a moaning chair. This will be your haven of despair and delight, where you

can rest and eye your fledgling craft, check your plans, pick out flaws before they become fatal, and dream of crackling campfires and foaming rapids.

Climate Considerations

Temperature and humidity are crucial to the resin curing process: the closer these conditions are to ideal, the clearer and tougher the finish on your canoe. For every 18-degrees F increase, the cure time can be cut in half. The longer the drying period, the greater the risk of contamination by dust and humidity. Even though the resin will eventually cure, it may be a less thorough polymerisation, weakening the sheath. On the other hand, extremely hot temperatures can be just as damaging. When a builder in California's Napa Valley laid up his canoe, the temperature soared to 90 degrees F, setting the resin almost as fast as he brushed it on. Ideal conditions are 60 to 70 degrees F, with a relative humidity of 45 to 65 percent. Even slightly cooler temperatures can make the resin hard to work and can produce a milky finish.

If you work in winter, be sure the space can be adequately heated. The temperature of the wood surface is more critical than the air temperature, so if you are heating the area just for lay-up, allow enough time for the hull to warm up. If you build during the hot summer months, prepare to forego some good paddling.

Average room lighting is not enough for boatbuilding. Hang several 200-watt bulbs directly over the work space. Intense direct light will eliminate shadows, helping you spot humps in the hull and assuring thorough epoxy coating of the cloth. One builder from North Augusta, Ontario, learned of the inadequacy of his gloomy workshop in a painful first-day launch. He thought his finished canoe looked great — until the unforgiving light of day made the resin runs and bare patches glaringly obvious for the first time.

Can You Breathe?

Ventilation is a major consideration when working with petrochemicals, especially if the fumes can seep from the workshop into living areas. Epoxy resin is not as foul as polyester resin, but some varnishes are much worse. The fumes can be cloying, choking off oxygen and causing headaches, nausea, dizziness and, occasionally, respiratory problems. Wood dust, especially from red cedar, can be just as hazardous. To keep the air clear, your boatshop should have operable windows for good cross-ventilation or an exhaust fan to suck out dust and fumes.

Options

Basement and garage are most often pressed into service as boatshops. Though basements offer better climate control, working in such close proximity to living

quarters can be harmful to more than your health — many woodstrip/epoxy canoes have taken shape in basements, to the tune of continuous objections from cohabitants. "I built in the basement, which was large, dry and well lit. It was suitable for me, though I'm not sure my parents would agree," reported one young Ottawa builder.

A garage may be a little cramped, but it solves fume and dust problems. Unless it is heated, your efforts will be limited to warm weather, which brings its own curse. Ruby-bellied mosquitoes permanently adorned the canoe of one enthusiast who built at the peak of the bug season. A summer garage boatshop may also bring out the onlookers, with their well-intentioned advice and cryptic assessments of your progress.

You can, if you must, build outside, though the canoe should be shaded. Direct sun can cause bubbles in uncured resin and cloud a finish coat. Even indoors, do not position the strongback where the sun's ultraviolet rays can fall directly on the hull for long periods of time. If it must be exposed to sunlight, cover the hull between sessions until it is protected with UV-shield varnish.

If the basement, garage, backyard and shed do not seem quite right for the job, you can follow the example of a Georgia canoeist, who, having assembled his boatbuilding materials, decided to add a sunroom/boatshop to his house

to have a proper place in which to create his canoe.

EQUIPMENT

A woodstrip canoe can be built with a bare minimum of tools. One teenager did the entire job with hand tools borrowed from a sympathetic and generous neighbour.

While the variety of equipment you have to work with has no direct bearing on the quality of the boat you build, you will do it in less time and with less frustration if you are properly outfitted.

Below is a list of the tools you will need. To get the most use out of them, they should be kept clean, sharp and easily accessible. A detailed list of required tools appears with each stage of the construction process.

Aside from conventional tools, you will occasionally need some equipment that is easily made from scraps of wood in your workshop. Directions are sprinkled throughout the text for handy devices like spring-fingers, push-sticks and sliding-rules. There are also instructions for several different "jigs," indispensable forms that hold a piece of work in place or guide a tool during repetitious operations. Though at first these may not seem worth the effort involved to make them, they will ease construction remarkably and, more important, will introduce you to the ingenious world of homemade tools.

THE RIGHT TOOLS

Tool	Use	Comments	Source
CUTTING TOOLS			
Crosscut handsaw	Cutting straight lines (building the strongback, cutting deck).		Hardware
Coping saw	Cutting out curves (moulds, decks, thwarts, scuppered gunwales).	Alternates: jig saw, sabre saw, band saw	Hardware
Table saw	Ripping planking, gunwales, keel; tapering trim.	Use hollow-ground combination or planer blade.	Hardware
Dovetail saw	Cutting hardwood trim and planking to length.	Won't mangle the ends as a crosscut might. Alternates: fine-tooth hacksaw, back saw.	Hardware
Utility knife	Trimming fibreglass cloth.	Alternate: jack knife.	Hardware
Scissors	Cutting fibreglass cloth.	Don't use your best pair.	Hardware
SHAPING AND FAIRING TOOLS			
Block plane	Fairing the hull and stems; shaping the ends of the planks where they meet at the bottom of the hull; fitting decks; shaping gunwales.	Alternative: spokeshave.	Woodwork supply Hardware
Jack plane	Dressing strongback planks; flattening hull where keel is attached; fitting decks; tapering gunwales and keel.	Alternate: Scrub plane, smoothing plane, block plane, though none are so long and heavy for flattening large areas.	Woodwork supply Hardware
Concave/convex plane	Fairing inside/outside of hull before lay-up.	Make your own.	Woodwork supply
Surform	Shaping curved surfaces; shaping cured epoxy.	Flat and curved bottom blades.	Hardware
Spokeshave	Smoothing compound curves as in shaping thwarts; fairing hull in tight spots where plane won't fit.	Very handy general workshop tool.	Woodwork supply
Cabinet scraper	Shaping hardwood.	Or sharpen one edge of half a hacksaw blade.	Woodwork supply
Rasp	Shaping and rounding edges on epoxy and trim.		Hardware
Router	Shaping trim; putting bead-and-cove edge on planking.	Supplier for bead-and-cove router cutters includes plans for table and jig.	Only one (page 144)
¾-inch chisel	Shaping and fitting.	Very useful.	Woodwork supply

Tool	Use	Comments	Source
Mill file	Smoothing metal edges on bolts, stem bands.		Woodwork supply
Sharpening stone	Maintaining keen edge on cutting tools.	Sharp tools are safer than dull ones.	Woodwork supply

SANDING TOOLS

Tool	Use	Comments	Source
Sanding block	Makes the most of your paper.	Buy shaped foam-backed rubber block or make from scrap wood.	Hardware
Orbital sander	Ideal for almost all sanding operations.	Fairly inexpensive, easily controlled power tool that will save a lot of time.	Hardware
Disc sander drill attachment	Sanding (with foam pad) outside and inside hull at turn of bilge where orbital can't fit.	Optional: practise controlling the machine before you apply it to the hull.	Hardware
Tack cloth	Wiping off sanded surfaces before applying finish.	Indispensable.	Hardware

FASTENING TOOLS

Tool	Use	Comments	Source
Staple gun	Fastening planks to stations and stitching planks together.	For use with ½″ or 9/16″ staples.	Hardware
Staple puller	Lifting staples.	Bend and pad end of flat screwdriver.	Hardware
Pliers	Removing staples once heads are exposed.		
Screwdrivers			
Drill and wood bits	Predrilling and countersinking screw holes.	Hand or powered drill; countersink bit to fit screw sizes.	Hardware
Counterbore and plug cutter	Counterboring screw holes for plugs in gunwales and seats.	Optional.	Hardware
C-clamps	Clamping stems, gunwales, decks and thwarts.	Minimum half-dozen 2″; more will speed up some jobs; make your own.	Hardware
Centre punch	Starting holes in brass stem band.		

FIBREGLASSING TOOLS

Tool	Use	Comments	Source
Mixing containers	Mixing resin and hardener.	Use paper coffee cups or small tin cans. You'll need six.	Hardware
Tin pie plate	Pouring out mixed resin before application.	Resin will not set up as fast in a thin layer.	
Stir sticks	Mixing resin and hardener.	Scraps of planking or tongue depressors.	Hardware
Syringe	Applying glue to bead-and-cove planking.	Curved nozzle.	Resin supplier

Tool	Use	Comments	Source
Glue roller	Applying glue to square-edge or shiplap planking.	4″ disposable paint roller	Paint store Hardware
Glue brushes	Gluing gunwales and trim.	Small, disposable.	Hardware Resin supplier
Epoxy roller	Applying last coats of epoxy; varnishing.	⅛″ foam; no substitutes.	Resin supplier
Squeegee	Scraping first coat resin and applying second coat.		Resin/body-shop supplier
Paint brush	Applying first and last coat epoxy and varnishing.	One 3″ short-bristled, cheap. One 3″, good quality.	Hardware Paint store
Mini-pumps	Dispensing resin and hardener; one shot of each gives 5:1 resin/hardener ratio.		Resin supplier
Putty knife	Cleaning up excess glue.		Hardware
Clean rags	Cleaning up.	Keep large supply on hand.	

MEASURING TOOLS

Tool	Use	Comments	Source
Metal tape measure			
Trysquare	Setting up mould.	Small (12″) metal.	
Level	Setting up mould.	2-foot size.	Hardware
Taut line	Determining long, straight lines.	Fine mason's line or wire fishing line.	Hardware

SAFETY

Tool	Use	Comments	Source
Dust mask	Machining and sanding.	Disposable model or one with replacement filters.	Paint or hardware store
Waterless hand cleaner	Protecting skin from solvents.		Epoxy/body-shop supplier
Gloves	Preventing epoxy skin irritation.	Disposable plastic; surgeon's gloves are ideal.	Hardware/paint store/drugstore
Fan	Controlling dust and fumes.	Window fan is acceptable.	
Basic first-aid kit			
Fire extinguisher		Appropriate for solvent and wood fires.	
Barrier cream	Prevents skin irritation.	Use with gloves when working with epoxy.	Epoxy supplier

MATERIALS

Wood is a traditional boatbuilding material, and there are purists who maintain it is still the best. Unfortunately, wood and water are not compatible in the long run.

The boatbuilder, unlike the cabinetmaker, must predict how wood's physical characteristics will be transformed by water. Successive cycles of moisture and dry storage weaken wood, accelerating its deterioration. Exposed to water, wood becomes dimensionally unstable, swelling and shrinking. Water, together with air, warmth and food, promotes rot fungi, the curse of wooden boatbuilders.

The *monocoque* structure described in this book has revolutionized wooden boatbuilding because it sandwiches wood inside a sheath of epoxy resin and fibreglass cloth, stabilizing its moisture content and eliminating dry rot. Thus protected, wood becomes a dimensionally stable and reliable building material. It is not a compromise, as some suggest, but an improvement, enhancing the natural buoyancy, strength and stiffness of wood with the durability of modern materials.

Wood

Wood not only gives your canoe its warm, sensuous beauty, it is the vital structural core of the monocoque system. Shaping itself smoothly to form, it offers good strength for its weight and volume.

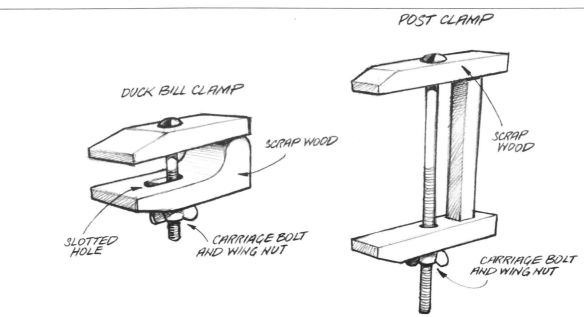

Homemade clamps can easily be made from scraps of wood — a wise economy measure for a project that uses dozens of clamps.

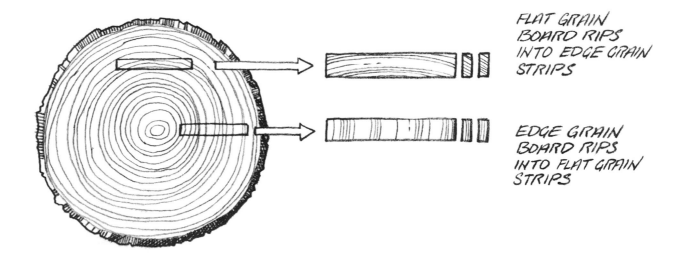

The grain of your wood strips affects their colour, texture and workability: edge grain strips are more uniform and easier to work; flat grain strips are harder to sand but are visually more interesting.

Above all, it is tough, naturally buoyant, and elastic. It is nature's own fibre-reinforced plastic, with cellulose fibre cells bonded together by lignin.

Different species of wood vary tremendously in their weight, strength and workability. There is no single species that is best for woodstrip/epoxy canoes. Your choice will depend on what you expect of your canoe, what is available locally and your budget. The epoxy sheath itself imposes little restriction since, unlike polyester, it bonds with most woods, however resinous or close-grained.

Throughout this book, wood sizes are given in actual or dressed dimensions, except in the materials list (page 67), where nominal dimensions are listed since this is how lumber is sold. The two compare as follows:

Nominal	Dressed
1"	¾"
2"	1½"
4"	3½"
6"	5½"
8"	7¼"
10"	9¼"

Planking

In selecting wood for your strips, the primary considerations are weight, workability, size and aesthetic appeal. Since the epoxy seals the planks from moisture and air, rot resistance is not important.

Lightness is usually prized in canoe wood, but if the boat will be used roughly or if it is not going to be portaged a lot, you may choose to sacrifice low weight for strength.

When lumber is sawn from a tree, it has either edge or flat grain (page 60). In terms of strength, this is not a major consideration because these planks are so small, but it does affect workability, colour and texture. Edge-grain strips are easier to sand and more uniform visually. Flat-grain strips are a little more dense, harder to sand, but more interesting in colour and texture.

The fewer knots and swirls in the wood, the straighter the grain, making the wood less prone to splitting and easier to rip on the saw. To get the maximum number of full-length strips with the fewest headaches, buy the best quality lumber you can find, with as few knots as possible.

The wood you buy should have no more than 12 percent moisture content, since dry wood is stronger, stiffer and lighter than wet. It does not matter whether it is air- or kiln-dried, although the latter is more brittle. Dry wood will rip cleanly; wet wood will fuzz as it goes through the saw. If the wood seems damp when you rip it, machine the strips and stack them for a week or so before planking the canoe.

Buy boards a foot longer than the canoe and as wide as practicable. Wider boards cost more but result in less waste when ripped into strips. A good compromise is 1 x 6-inch lumber, dressed to ¾ inch. A 16-foot canoe will require about 50 board feet.

Instead of buying dimensional lumber, you can buy the planking precut. (See Sources, page 143.) It will cost more but will eliminate a lot of frustration. If you buy precut planking, look for a supplier that offers bead-and-cove edging.

Trim

Because the trim forms the structural skeleton of the canoe, hardwood should be used. Dense species like oak and ash can be pared down for sleek lines without sacrificing strength. The specific gravity of hardwoods varies considerably, so weight can be cut simply by choosing a lighter species. Since trim accounts for up to half the weight of a canoe, you will be grateful for any savings when you hoist the boat over long portages.

Finding hardwood in lengths long enough for gunwales might be difficult, though short pieces can be glued with a scarf joint (page 73). As in planking, look for clear, straight grain; when you try to twist a gunwale into its compound bend, it will break at the knots. Beyond its practical function, trim can be the vehicle for those frivolous aesthetic touches that set your canoe apart from all others, be it a coaming of exotic purple heartwood against a golden deck of bird's eye maple or a creamy sitka spruce inwale accented with black-cherry scuppers. Where weight, expense and clear, long lengths are not an issue, select woods for their eye appeal and for their fine finish alone.

The woods listed in the chart are only the most common species used in canoes. The choice is unlimited. Peterborough builders used butternut to trim and plank canoes and often added a racing stripe of black walnut. Rushton shaped his thwarts in maple. White cedar is a prime canoe wood, but almost impossible to get, perhaps because in the 1880s, it was considered the best of all breeds for lightweight watercraft and was exported to discriminating boatbuilders all over the world.

Finding good wood has always been a challenge for boatbuilders. Rushton himself had to turn to West Coast lumber as an alternative to dwindling Eastern supplies. Clear, long timbers are even more elusive today.

Local lumberyards may have the wood, but prices will be high and selection limited. Specialty wood stores offer the best quality and selection at premium prices. If you can find a wholesale lumber dealer who will sell retail, the price and selection will be tops, but the quality will be hard to judge since the boards will not be dressed. Lumber mills offer the best price and maintain the tradition of using local woods, but quality will depend on timber stands in the area. The lumber will not be dressed, and the moisture content may be unpredictable.

Wherever you buy it, take the time to select your wood carefully. Look for long, straight, clear planks that are dressed to an even thickness and free of gouges, splits or planer skips. As you sort through the stack, keep the colour of your canoe in mind. Be picky — this wood is going to keep you and yours afloat long after that impatient clerk has retired.

Resin

In the monocoque structure, resin is the vital link between cloth and wood. It is more than just a glue and a glassy shell — it penetrates the core, bonding wood, cloth and plastic into a cohesive whole.

There are two major types used in boat building — polyester and epoxy. Both are petrochemical-based liquids that become solid when a catalyst or curing agent is added. When I started to build strip canoes more than a decade ago, I brushed polyester over the planking but soon found it inadequate as a sheathing system.

Polyester was the first partner for fibreglass cloth in the FRP (fibre-reinforced plastic) process. Used alone with fibreglass, it produces excellent canoes, but applied over wood, its drawbacks are obvious.

Polyester resin does not bond well to any kind of wood and will not cure at all over the knots and heartwood of resinous species. Diluted with styrene to make it easier to handle, polyester shrinks as it cures, creating high surface tension and tiny pores that invite water vapour to penetrate into the wood. Little more than a glassy coating, it will separate from the core at the slightest impact. If woodstrip/resin canoes have a reputation as delicate boats, it is mostly due to the inferiority of polyester resin.

Epoxy is more expensive than polyester, but its advantages more than justify the cost. Unlike the linear chain polyesters, epoxy is composed of multidirectional interlocking-molecule chains. Composed of 100 percent solids, it shrinks only imperceptibly as it cures.

Because it is compatible with wood's own natural resins, epoxy bonds chemically as well as mechanically with all species, which means that builders can use less epoxy and cloth, dramatically reducing weight and costs without having to flinch every time their canoes scrape a rock.

Properly formulated and applied, epoxy has proved superior to polyester in flexibility, resilience and impact resistance. In a test reported in *Woodenboat* magazine in July/August 1977, a coat of epoxy, though half as thick, had twice the impact resistance of polyester on wood.

Although epoxy smells sweet and mild (I liken it to the aroma of baked apples), it can be toxic when absorbed through the skin: People who are highly sensitive may break out in a rash. As a precaution, it should never be handled without barrier cream and gloves.

Not all epoxies will give your wood a clear, tough sheath. There are as many formulations of the resins as there are applications. The best epoxy is the one with the fewest restrictions and the most predictability. When mixed, it should be thin enough to saturate the cloth and surface wood fibres, but thick enough to hang on a vertical plane without sagging or running. You should be able to recoat within a few hours and sand within a day. (Some I have tested were still rubbery after two weeks.) Finally, the epoxy should cure with good clarity, adding no objectionable tint to the wood. One brand was fine over dark planking, but turned Sitka spruce an ugly greenish yellow.

There are a handful of epoxies designed specifically for marine use. Bear Mountain Canoe Company has tested most, and of these, WEST SYSTEM brand epoxy by Gougeon Brothers Inc. seems best suited for the monocoque method. (See Sources page 143.)

Always buy WEST SYSTEM 206 slow hardener for sheathing a woodstrip canoe. The fast formula tends to set before it can saturate the fibreglass and wood fibres, and it cures so quickly that maintaining a wet edge is impossible.

For a 16-foot canoe, you will need roughly 15 pounds (1½ U.S. gallons) of resin and the appropriate amount of hardener. (Buy the calibrated pumps that dispense the resin and hardener in accurate 5:1 proportion.) This should provide three coats inside and out, with enough left over to glue the trim.

Stored in a cool place, resin and hardener have a shelf life of about a year. When you are ready to lay-up your canoe, mix and apply the epoxy according to manufacturer's instructions, with strict attention to your workshop conditions (page 56).

Cloth Reinforcement

Although wood and epoxy alone would give your canoe good end-to-end strength, the cloth reinforcement ties the strips together across the grain, effectively taking the place of ribs. The cloth also ensures that a minimum consistent thickness of epoxy is applied on the hull.

Fibreglass cloth is a convenient, effective, relatively inexpensive reinforcement for woodstrip canoes. It is made from fine continuous filaments of molten glass, spun into thread and woven together as cloth. When wetted out, it becomes completely transparent, revealing the beauty of the wood.

Sold by the running yard, fibreglass cloth comes in various widths and weights. I recommend a single sheet of 6-ounce x 50- or 60-inch cloth the length of the canoe for the inside of the hull, and a single sheet a foot longer than the canoe for the outside. If you are more interested in weight than strength, buy a lighter (4-ounce) cloth. On the other hand, if your boat will be put to hard use, you may want to increase the cloth weight in some areas, gaining extra strength at the expense of clarity.

THE RIGHT WOODS

Name	Advantages	Disadvantages	Use
Western red cedar (*Thuya plicata*)	Light; workable with hand tools; good colour range; available in long lengths; close, straight, even grain.	Red cedar is a little more brittle than white.	Ideal for planking.
Sitka spruce (*Picea sitchensis*)	Very good strength-to-weight ratio; sapwood pale yellow, heartwood brown; available in long clear lengths; does not sand as fast as cedar, but tougher, nearly nonresinous; elastic; straight, even grain.	Adds 5 to 6 pounds more weight to 16-foot canoe than cedar; does not take much abrasion.	Ideal for planking, yokes and spars; use on hull bottom and high-stress areas for extra strength; good for trim if weight a primary consideration.
Redwood (*Pinus sylvestris*)	Workability comparable to cedar; fairly dark colour; available in long clear lengths; straight grain.	Heavier than cedar; fairly brittle; moderately resinous; soft, subject to wear.	Suitable for planking.
Ash (*Fraxinus*)	Good bendability; strong for its weight; wears well; fair workability; very tough and elastic.	For high finish, use filler; not durable when exposed to weather; coarse texture.	Ideal for trim (keel, gunwales, seat frames, decks, stems).
Oak (*Quercus*)	White more bendable than red; red coarse, white fine textured; attractive grain; tough, durable.	Poor workability with hand tools; hard to get good finish; open grain, use filler; heavy; hard to glue.	Suitable for trim.
Cherry (*Prunus*)	Beautiful; good workability; reasonably light for strength; ages well; takes finish well.	Does not bend as well as ash; not readily available, especially in long lengths.	Suitable for trim.
Mahogany (more than 60 different tropical species are sold under this name)	Good workability with hand tools; lighter than cherry; available in long lengths; highly figured, brown to red.	Open grain, use filler for good finish; hard to find good quality; some types susceptible to splits.	Suitable for trim; Honduras & African mahogany are most desirable.

Although all fibreglass cloth looks the same, manufacturers use different chemical finishes that can affect adhesion. Some fabric is treated with a chemical coupling agent to improve the resin-fibre bond. Whatever system you use, buy the fibreglass fabric recommended by the resin manufacturer or supplier.

Cloth adds toughness to a canoe, but it also adds weight, so builders are always experimenting with new "miracle" fabrics that claim to be light *and* durable. Unfortunately, most have proved unsuitable for woodstrip/epoxy canoes.

A modacrylic fabric like Dynel withstands scuffing and abrasion very well. Half the weight of fibreglass, it drapes softly and is easily saturated with resin. It is highly absorbent, however, puffing up to twice the thickness of fibreglass, with a rough, hard-to-sand surface. Despite superior abrasion resistance, its impact resistance is the same as fibreglass.

A polypropylene fabric, such as Vectra or Versatex, weighs a third as much as fibreglass but has 15 times the tear strength and twice the impact and abrasion resistance. It takes contours well, but being lightweight, tends to "float" on the resin and fuzzes badly when sanded. In a woodstrip canoe, the weave will become visible after a few seasons of exposure.

An aramid fabric like Kevlar-49 has such a high tensile strength that you need carbide-tipped cutting tools. Its impact resistance lies somewhere between fibreglass and polypropylene. It does not work particularly well with wood, remains a yellow-brown colour when wetted out and, at 10 times the price of fibreglass, has no place in woodstrip canoe construction.

Generally, the alternatives are more expensive and less transparent than fibreglass. Most important, they are much more elastic than wood, flexing greatly under stress. For woodstrip construction, any cloth should have a stretch factor close to that of the wood core, so the two will work together under impact, each compounding the strength of the other.

At this writing, I consider fibreglass the best mate for wood and epoxy in the average cruising canoe. If you want extra protection in the high-abuse zone below the waterline, lay a narrow panel of polypropylene over the keel-line. The fibreglass laid over top eliminates any floating or sanding problems.

Glue

Among the vast array of adhesives available today, only a few are appropriate for building woodstrip canoes. The glue that holds the planks together must bond with little clamping pressure and have some gap-filling properties. It should be easy to mix and spread, have a comfortably long pot life, but dry reasonably fast under average conditions. It must be easily sanded, compatible with epoxy resin and relatively nontoxic, since

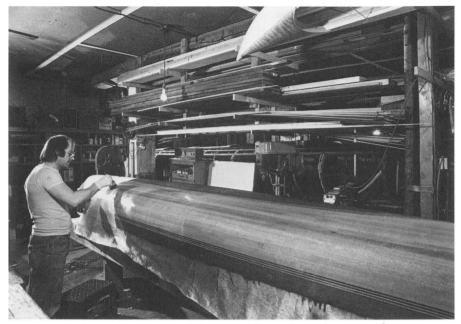

A neat workshop, with the wood strips stored flat and out of the way yet handy to the mould, expedites construction.

Among the specialized tools for applying the glue and resin are syringes, mini-pumps and the all-important squeegee, **far right**.

you will be exposed to its fumes and dust. Since it will not be encased in epoxy, glue for the trim must be completely waterproof. The types described below are commonly available from hardware stores or marine suppliers.

Urea Formaldehyde Resin Glue

Also known as plastic resin glue, this is sold as a light brownish powder that is mixed with water to the consistency of cream. It has a long pot life (3 to 4 hours) and will bond with hand pressure. Though not as good as epoxy, its gap-filling properties are adequate, and it sands beautifully. Curing temperatures are not critical, but it is moderately toxic and should be used with gloves. Because it is water-resistant, not waterproof, it is most appropriate for planking, where it is sealed in epoxy. It dries straw-coloured and can be wiped off with water within 20 minutes. Although sometimes hard to find, it is the traditional boatbuilding glue and my first choice for gluing strips because it is easy to work with and inexpensive. Note: Two-part urea adhesives have entirely different characteristics.

Solvent: water
Required: 1½ pounds
Recommended: planking

Epoxy Resin Glue

Developed during World War II, epoxy was used by the aircraft industry a decade before boatbuilders discovered it. Its superior bond makes it the most promising, though most expensive, boatbuilding adhesive. Colourless and waterproof, the strong flexible bond does not require a precise fit or clamping pressure. Its gap-filling capacity is unexcelled, because the resin film between surfaces actually makes the joint stronger. Though correct temperature and humidity are important for proper curing, epoxy glue sands extremely well when hard. To use as glue, blend resin and hardener in the correct ratio, stir well, then add two or three pinches of microfiber filler. These fine cotton fibres thicken the epoxy slightly, giving it extra strength and body without affecting its ability to penetrate the wood. Epoxy glue has a pot life of about a half-hour, a liability when gluing planking. Glued joints harden enough in 6 to 8 hours for clamps to be removed. Before it sets, excess epoxy should be wiped off with a cloth dipped in solvent. Microfiber filler is nontoxic, but always wear gloves because the epoxy itself can cause skin irritation. This glue is ideal for trim but tends to be too messy for planking because of the finicky handling required. It can also be used as a wood filler by adding sanding dust to improve body and to colour match the wood.

Solvent: acetone or lacquer
  thinner
Required: 1½ quarts for planking,
  small bag microfibers
Recommended: trim

All-Purpose Wood Glue

White carpenter glues like Bondfast, Weldwood and Elmer's are cheap, widely available and nontoxic, and they require no mixing. They are water-resistant but not waterproof. They are the easiest to handle and clean but are the most difficult to sand. The glue remains rubbery when cured and smears with the friction heat of sanding, gumming up the paper. You have to be especially cautious with power sanders since the wood smooths faster than the glue. Its gap-filling properties are adequate.

Solvent: water
Required: 1½ quarts
Acceptable

Resorcinol Resin

Introduced in the early 1940s, this waterproof glue is sold as a water-soluble powder or a two-part system of liquid resin and powdered catalyst. Since it requires a precise fit, high pressure and warm temperatures for a good bond, it is not suitable for strip gluing. It can be used for waterproof joints in the trim, however, and is ideal for gluing oak. Besides being fairly expensive, it cures to a brownish purple colour which, if not part of the design, can be objectionable.

Not recommended.

Varnish

Varnish is more than cosmetic. It protects epoxy from the sun's damaging ultraviolet rays and keeps water from penetrating the trim.

Buy a high-quality spar varnish with a UV (ultraviolet) shield. Made from tung oil, with hardeners and pigments added, spar varnish is easy to work with and has a pleasant smell. It is expensive, however, and this is a clear case of getting what you pay for. Buy top quality, and expect to pay a premium price.

Do not substitute standard polyurethane varnish. Although cheaper, it is brittle and has a tendency to peel and yellow, and it probably will not have UV filters.

Some of the two-part polyurethanes are worth considering. They are tougher but are very expensive and can be toxic if sprayed.

Solvent: mineral spirits
Required: 1 quart

Solvents

You will need two different solvents — one for epoxy and one for varnish.

With epoxy, the solvent is used to clean uncured resin from your tools and mop up spills. You will also need it to wipe down the surface of the hull before applying resin coats.

Lacquer thinner, acetone and methylene chloride are all good epoxy solvents. Acetone is an excellent cleaner, but it is expensive and evaporates quickly. Methylene chloride is not as flammable as the others, but it is expensive and not readily available. Lacquer thinner, though not as effective as the other two, will do the job nicely and is both cheaper and easy to find. Buy it from an automobile body-shop supplier. It comes in several grades, but since you are using it for cleaning up, buy the cheapest. A quart should be sufficient.

For varnishing, buy a quart of mineral spirits. Varsol, made by Esso, is good but buy the cheapest.

Polyclens is an excellent brush cleaner that is worth keeping in the workshop all the time. Pour an inch of the pleasant-smelling pink liquid in a can and soak your brush, after removing the bulk of the resin or varnish with solvent. Wash under the tap, and your brush will come out like new.

Do not use these solvents for cleaning your hands. They are irritants and strip your skin of its natural protective oils. Instead, keep a can of waterless hand cleaner in the shop or use soap and water.

Abrasives

It is hard to say how much sandpaper you are going to need, but the best place to buy it is at a body-shop supplier, where you can get it in bulk instead of high-priced packets of two or three sheets.

The brand does not matter as long as you have the right grit. You will need a medium #80-grit aluminium-oxide paper for the epoxy-sanding, fine #120-grit and very fine #220-grit for finishing and #150- to #240-grit waterproof paper for wet-sanding.

Stem Band

The brass stem band is a protective device that gives your canoe a natty, nautical look. If you have a keel, you will need enough brass to cover the full length of the boat, stem to stem, plus an inch or two extra at each deck. It comes in 10-foot lengths, 3/8 x 3/16-inch. You can substitute aluminum, but it is not as tough, nor does it look as traditional. You may have some trouble finding brass banding, but the effect is worth the effort. (See Sources, page 143.)

Fasteners

Ever since the first primitive boat moved past the one-log stage, man has had to use his ingenuity to tie its parts together. The Norse used rawhide strips, the Romans hammered bronze and copper pins, and North American Indians laced black spruce roots. Gluing the planks together and sealing them in resin eliminates much of the need for fasteners, but you still have to tie the gunwales, thwarts, seats and decks to the hull.

Except in the strongback, screws must be noncorrosive, which eliminates the common steel variety. Brass screws are the traditional choice; the colour melds beautifully with the canoe's wood hues, but they are soft and require extra care to prevent the heads from twisting off. (This can be avoided by first twisting in a steel screw to cut threads in the wood.) Bronze is a tougher traditional screw but

hard to find. Stainless-steel screws are the easiest to use and can usually be found at a marine supply.

You will also need staples with a medium crown (½-inch) for fastening planking to the stations. Instead of staples, 1-inch finishing nails can be used.

COST

Price often starts out as the primary motivation for building a woodstrip/epoxy canoe, and rightly so.

You will definitely save money by building, rather than buying, this type of canoe, which, in 1983, sold for prices ranging from $1,500 to $2,500.

Even buying the most expensive lumber, you should be able to build any of the designs in this book for less than $400 (at 1983 material prices). That is a significant saving, even without considering the priceless personal touches you build into your own boat. As most builders will tell you, their dollar investment was more than repaid long before their canoe took its maiden voyage.

Below is a shopping list of all the materials needed to complete this project, together with their dimensions and quantities. Check the Sources (page 143), and shop around for the best quality at the best price. Quote it to friends and partners who question your sanity in investing 150 to 250 hours in a slender double-ended watercraft.

SAFETY

The expression "safety is no accident" may be a cliché, but it is true nevertheless. The pleasure of building your own canoe will soon dissipate if a preventable accident occurs.

All the usual safety precautions of a home workshop apply to canoebuilding. Keep flammable liquids tightly capped in a safe place, and do not smoke. Keep your work area well lit, clean and organized. Work at a comfortable height whenever possible. Keep a fire extinguisher and first aid kit within easy reach at all times.

Working with epoxy imposes its own extra measure of caution. Do not let children or pets in your work area during lay-up. The process is messy enough without having to worry about small bodies. Ventilate the area well. Deposit resin and solvent wastes in a metal can and store it outside away from combustibles.

Resin dust can also be highly flammable. One builder lit a cigarette after sanding down his fibreglassed hull and snapped the lighter shut on his knee. The dust on his clothes caught fire, enveloping him in a flash of flame. Luckily, he escaped with only singed body hair and a racing heart.

Epoxy resins and hardeners have a reputation as skin sensitizers, though WEST SYSTEM epoxy seems to have relatively low toxicity. The hardener is a more serious irritant than the resin, but skin contact should be rigorously avoided with both. Never handle either without applying barrier cream and wearing rubber gloves. Also, take care to protect your eyes from splashes of hardener by wearing safety glasses. If you do get some in your eye, flush it out with water for a least 15 minutes, and see a doctor. If you develop a rash while working with epoxy, stop using it, and consult your physician.

During epoxy lay-up, wear old clothes. What you spill will be a life-long memento. Wear a dust mask or respirator to filter out the fumes and particles produced by machining wood and applying and sanding epoxy and varnish. Goggles, if kept clean, will protect your eyes during the ripping process.

At the beginning of each stage in canoe construction, the recommended safety equipment is listed – take the precautions advised and make this boatbuilding project a successful and safe one.

THE RIGHT MATERIALS

LUMBER
Strongback:
   Two 2" x 10" x canoe length of kiln-dried spruce for T-beam
   Two 2" x 10" x 32" kiln-dried spruce for legs
   Two 2" x 4" x 24" kiln-dried spruce for feet
   Eight 1" x 1" x 9½" softwood cornerblocks
Moulds:
   Two sheets 4" x 8" x ⅜" particle board
   One 2" x 2" x 9½" softwood station block per station
   Four 1" x 1" softwood cornerblocks just less than stem height
Stem:
   Three ¼" x 1" lengths of hardwood, 40" to 50" (length of stem), per stem
Planking:
   50 board feet of 1" x 6" softwood, 12" longer than canoe
Inwales:
   Two 1" x desired width hardwood, 12" longer than canoe
Outwales:
   Two 1" x desired width hardwood, 12" longer than canoe
Decks:
   Two 1" x desired width hardwood x length of deck
Thwarts:
   One or two 1" x 2½" to 3" hardwood x width of canoe
Seats:
   Two 1" x 1½" x 7' hardwood
   Two ¾" x 12" hardwood dowels
FASTENERS
Strongback:
   One box 3" #8 steel screws or one box 3½" common nails
   One box 1½" #6 steel screws or one box 2" common nails
Setting up Mould:
   One box 2" steel screws
Planking:
   One box ½" staples for bead-and-cove OR
   Two boxes 1" staples for square edge or shiplap
Inwales:
   One box ½" #4 flat head noncorrosive screws
Outwales:
   One box 1½" #6 to #8 flat head noncorrosive screws

Decks:
   Two 1" x desired width hardwood x length of deck
Seats:
   Four 3/16" x 4" to 6" carriage bolts or machine screws per seat
Thwarts:
   Four 3/16 x 2" carriage bolts or machine screws per thwart
Stem:
   One ⅜" x 3/16" metal band x desired length
SHEATHING
Fibreglass Cloth (6 oz.):
   One piece 60" wide x canoe length for inside hull
   One piece 60" wide x canoe length plus 12" for outside hull
Epoxy Resin:
   15 pounds (1½ gallons)
WEST SYSTEM **206 Hardener:**
   As specified by manufacturer
Spar Varnish:
   2 quarts
GLUING
Planking:
   1½ pounds plastic resin OR
   Epoxy resin and one small bag microfibers
Trim and Filler:
   Resin and microfibers
SOLVENTS
   One quart lacquer thinner for epoxy
   One quart mineral spirits for varnish
   One pint Polyclens for brushes
MISCELLANEOUS
   Two to three sheets of largest-size carbon paper for moulds
   One roll ¾" masking tape
   One bar paraffin for mould release
   One package disposable paint filters for varnish
   24 sheets #80 sandpaper
   24 sheets #120 sandpaper
   6 sheets #220 sandpaper
   6 sheets #240 wet sandpaper
   Pencil
   Ballpoint pen

MATERIAL MATTERS

Machining the Wood

Are we quite sure that there is no feeling in the "heart of oak," no sentiment under bent birch ribs; that a canoe, in fact, has no character?

— John MacGregor

Having chosen the design of your canoe and bought all the necessary materials, there is a real temptation to plunge ahead into the construction of the hull. It is possible, of course, to swing into action, but in doing so, you will find that progress on the canoe is repeatedly delayed as you stop to machine the parts for the next stage of construction. Because the making of parts can account for up to a quarter of your total boatbuilding hours, some builders prefer to do all the machining at once, so that when the hull is complete, there is no delay fitting in the seats, thwarts, deck and other parts that transform the hull into a canoe.

I prefer to make all the miscellaneous parts first and then work as quickly as possible without interruption. A novice, on the other hand, might prefer to prepare the planking, inwales and outwales prior to starting work on the hull and then build the seats, decks and thwarts after the body of the canoe has been built.

One Ottawa man leisurely machined the parts and prepared the mould one winter, built the hull the next and happily launched his new canoe on a sunny May morning more than two years after beginning his project. It all depends on the pace and priorities of the builder.

For convenience's sake, all the machining has been gathered within this single chapter. The specifications for each part, of course, will be dictated by the size and shape of your canoe, but there are few other restrictions. Armed with what you learn from this chapter, you should be able to let your imagination wander through all sorts of possibilities.

In each section, the machining instructions begin with a basic approach, then proceed through increasingly interesting variations to the most exquisitely complex. The difference between approaches is usually not dependent on woodworking skill so much as patience and dedication to your personal concept of the ideal canoe.

Ripping the Planking

This is the first real step in building your canoe – slicing those long hefty boards into thin, supple strips that will bend to an elegant shape and eventually sustain you through heavy waves or swirling rapids.

Ripping the planks is not difficult, providing you take the time to set up the equipment and work area first. Your overriding aim in this process is to produce long planks of uniform ¼-inch thickness along their full length.

This can be done using either a table saw or a band saw. The band saw is a little safer and easier to operate, but unless its blade is wide, it has a tendency to wander. Most home workshops have a table saw, which will give you a nice, smooth cut if you are careful and use a sharp, hollow-ground com-

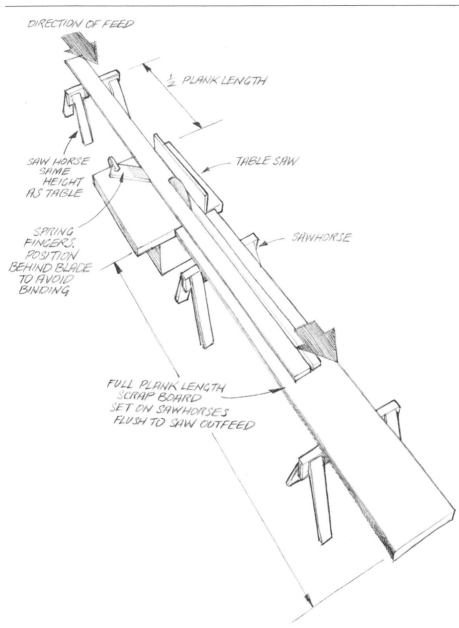

DIRECTION OF FEED

½ PLANK LENGTH

SAW HORSE SAME HEIGHT AS TABLE

TABLE SAW

SPRING FINGERS. POSITION BEHIND BLADE TO AVOID BINDING

SAWHORSE

FULL PLANK LENGTH SCRAP BOARD SET ON SAWHORSES FLUSH TO SAW OUTFEED

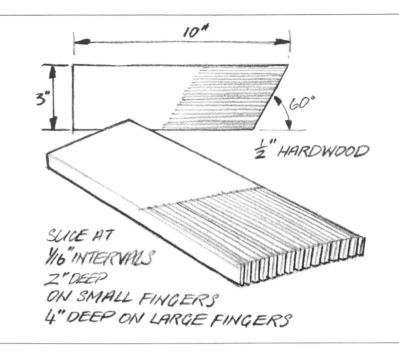

10"

3"

60°

½" HARDWOOD

SLICE AT
1/16" INTERVALS
2" DEEP
ON SMALL FINGERS
4" DEEP ON LARGE FINGERS

Above: *Arrange a support system of sawhorses to keep the planking level when ripping boards into strips.* **Top right:** *Spring fingers clamped to the saw table act like an extra hand, pressing the plank firmly against the fence while the builder feeds the plank through the blade,* **bottom**.

bination blade or a thin planer blade. The latter will give you better strips with less waste, but use it only if the wood is perfectly dry.

These long boards will sag and bind the blade unless they are supported. Still, it is safer and more accurate to make preparations to do the job alone than try to work with (and against) a helper. To do this, set up a sawhorse the same height as the table, about 8 feet from the infeed side of the saw. On the opposite side, set up two more sawhorses, with a board or piece of plywood between them. Butt the board flush to the outfeed side of the table to support the plank as it leaves the blade (page 70). With this system, you can control the plank and keep it level as you push it through the saw.

The ripping process will flow more smoothly if you clean the saw table before you start, and rub it with paraffin. Set the blade slightly above the thickness of the wood (although a hollow-ground blade should be raised a little higher for extra clearance, as the blade is thinner near the centre). Set the rip fence at ¼ inch, almost parallel to the blade but offset fractionally away from the back of the blade to prevent binding and kickback.

For consistent thickness, the plank must be pressed tightly against the fence. This is dangerous work for human hands, especially as the board gets thinner. Rather than lose fingers, and for greater control and safety, make a

set of spring fingers, sometimes called a "featherboard" (right). Cut at an angle one end of an 8-to-10-inch length of 3 x ½-inch hardwood, then slice it through at 1/16-inch intervals. Rub the ends of the fingers with paraffin to reduce friction, and use a large C-clamp to fasten it to the saw table, so the fingers exert pressure on the board just before it meets the saw blade, holding it tightly against the fence.

With spring fingers and lumber supports in place, begin to push the board through the saw blade. Proceed cautiously at an even rate, watching for gaps between the board and fence. If the plank wanders and causes a thin spot in the strip, break it out as soon as it is through the saw. Don't force the board: the blade may bind or the motor stall and overheat. Let the cutting of the blade set the speed.

When the end of the board reaches the table, use a push stick (right) to guide it through the blade to the other side. This will give you the longest consistent strip possible. When they are all cut, store the strips where they will not be trampled.

This is an incredibly dusty operation, as for every two planks you rip, one is blown away in sawdust, so wear a mask at all times, and be sure the shop is well ventilated. It is also a good idea to wear safety goggles or glasses. Remember to keep them clean.

If you do not want to rip your own planking, you can buy it precut or pay a local cabinetmaker to

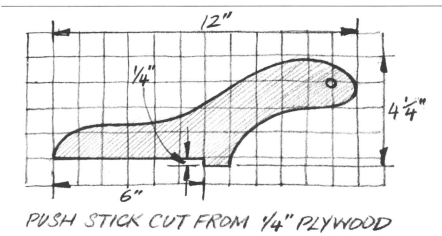

PUSH STICK CUT FROM ¼" PLYWOOD

A push stick provides a margin of safety when feeding wood through a table saw. Cut one from ¼-inch plywood.

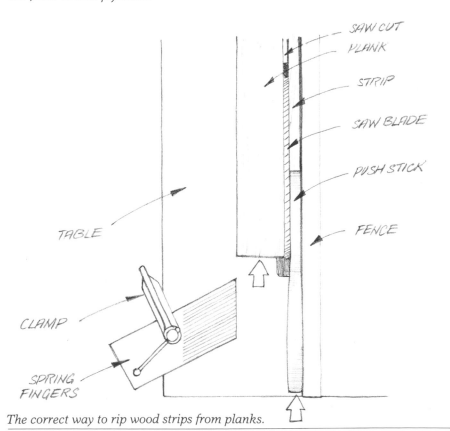

The correct way to rip wood strips from planks.

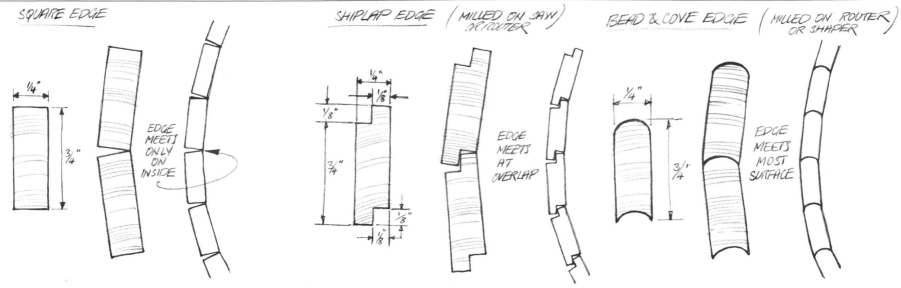

SQUARE EDGE

SHIPLAP EDGE (MILLED ON SAW OR ROUTER)

BEAD & COVE EDGE (MILLED ON ROUTER OR SHAPER)

1/4"

3/4"

EDGE MEETS ONLY ON INSIDE

1/4"

1/8"

1/8"

3/4"

1/8"

1/8"

EDGE MEETS AT OVERLAP

1/4"

3/4"

EDGE MEETS MOST SURFACE

The three edges of planking; although hardest to machine, bead-and-cove edging provides the ideal gluing surface.

rip the boards for you. Whichever route you take, be sure to end up with long, absolutely uniform ¼-inch planks.

Machining the Planking

There are serious drawbacks to using this square-edge planking as is. Because they cannot be interlocked, it is hard to keep the planks in line when they are being laid across the moulds. Even with a fortune in temporary staples punched between the stations, the strips will want to spring apart.

Because the hull is a continuous curve, the butting edges will not mate along their full width. This creates gaps, especially on sharp curves, and reduces gluing surface so much that planks may pop apart when staples are pulled. For an idea of the problems that occur,

hoist a butt-planked canoe over your head at midday, and chances are that shafts of sunlight will pierce the hull.

The amount of gluing surface can be improved on square-edge planking if you bevel the edge of each strip to mate with the one below. This requires a fair amount of skill, because it is a rolling bevel and entails a great deal of trial-and-error fitting.

A better approach is to machine each plank with a shiplap edge that locks the strips together in one direction. Although the gluing surface is increased, the joints may still need a few between-station staples to keep them from separating.

For a shiplap edge, set both the saw blade and fence at ⅛ inch. (Screw a false wooden fence to the saw fence to prevent damage if the

blade hits it.) Press the strip against the fence with spring fingers clamped to the table. Make another short (3-to-4-inch) set of spring fingers and clamp it to the fence, pressing down on the plank. Push the first strip through, taking a ⅛-inch notch out of the bottom of the strip. When the first strip reaches the table, use another strip to push it completely through the blade. Continue the uninterrupted flow of strips until one edge is milled on all of the planks. Then flip them over and do the other edge.

Beyond this method, however, planking with a bead-and-cove edge will give you the smoothest, tightest joints. Regardless of the angle at which they come together, the bead and cove lock the strips together in both directions and

provide maximum gluing surface. Although somewhat more fragile, bead-and-cove edging reduces stapling, frustration and fairing time. One builder, after working with butt planking, decided to switch to bead and cove for his next canoe. Using a moulding cutterhead and knives on his table saw, he machined all the planking in a half hour, saving himself hours of fitting and fairing.

The bead and cove can also be milled with cutters designed for use with ¼-inch router bits. There is only one North American source (page 143), but the cutters include plans for a router jig so that both bead-and-cove edges can be cut simultaneously. You can also mill the edge with Rockwell's three-wing cutters fitted for a ½-inch shaper. If you machine the two edges separately, do the bead-edge of all planks first and then the cove. The latter is fragile; handle as little as possible.

Machining the Keel

Keels are generally made from hardwood as this part of the canoe gets most of the hard knocks. There are many types and sizes of keels, but the method of machining and fastening is basically the same. The keel described here is appropriate for all the canoe designs in this book.

Choose the straightest and clearest hardwood plank you can find, and rip a ¾ x ⅞-inch piece, about a foot shorter than the overall length of the boat. This must be shaped into a triangular piece with a ⅞-inch base, where it attaches to the hull, and a ⅜-inch seat for the brass keel band. To do this, draw the angles on the end of the keel, as shown at right. Set the saw to the same angle and cut a piece of scrap lumber to test the accuracy. Cut the keel, then clean up the saw cuts with block plane or cabinet scraper. Sand the angled sides with #120 paper, keeping the edges of the keel sharp.

Machining the Gunwales

On a canoe, gunwales have little to do with artillery but everything to do with structure — they tie the boat together end to end. Projecting beyond the hull both inside and out, they absorb and distribute stresses along their entire length. They must be tough enough to withstand the flexion of a hull in rough water, strong enough to support the hanging seats, yet light and supple enough to take the long compound bend of the sheer-line. They can be as simple as square lengths of wood or carved and tapered to add an elegant touch of finesse to your boat.

The gunwale dimensions for each canoe can be scaled from the line drawings. Sometimes, it is difficult to find hardwood long enough for the job, but this can be overcome by gluing two short pieces with a scarf joint, provided they are similar in colour and grain. Mark both with an angle seven inches long for every inch of thickness. Cut each roughly to size on the table saw and dress to the line with a plane. Because the open grain absorbs a lot of glue, apply epoxy to both surfaces until no more will soak in, then clamp the joint together. By attaching the scarf joint to the hull so that one end lays on top of the other, it will be virtually invisible from above.

Inwales

Inwales make up the inside half of the gunwales and can range from subtle slivers of trim to elaborately carved handrails.

The lightest and simplest inwales are shaped from a solid piece of ⅜ x ¾-inch hardwood cut a few inches longer than the sheer-line. Although too narrow to hang seats from, they are ideal for small, one-man Nessmuk-style canoes, where the paddler sits in the bottom of the

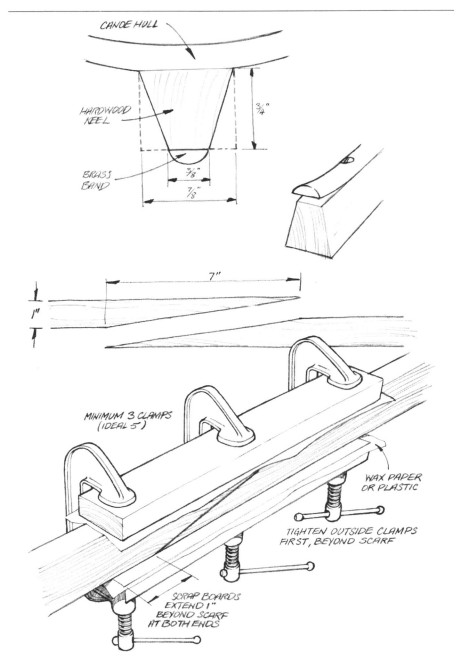

Above: *Keel is shaped to take a narrow stem band.* **Below:** *The scarf joint is ideal for joining two pieces of trim.*

hull. After they are fitted, the edges are rounded so water is not trapped inside the canoe when the hull is overturned.

Solid ¾-inch square inwales are the strongest, best suited for large, rugged canoes, but they are heavy and chunky-looking and prevent water from draining out of the boat when it is overturned. Scuppered or slotted, inwales overcome the drainage problem, and I prefer them because they are reminiscent of those on traditional cedarstrips, where the narrow ribs created rhythmic spaces between the hull and inwale. Scuppered inwales have the strength of solid inwales but can reduce total canoe weight by as much as a pound each. The slots are great for lashing gear.

If you choose the airy elegance of scuppered inwales, indulge your creative whims in the size and placement of the slots: elegant, long handrails or closely spaced eyelets. They can extend the full length of the sheer-line or stop before the decks (right). In any case, draw the design first, making sure that there is solid wood where the seats and thwarts will hang.

The slots can be carved from a solid inwale or formed by gluing blocks between a narrower inwale and the hull. Both methods are fiddly and time-consuming, but the final effect is worth it.

For a carved inwale, draw ¼-inch-wide slots on a ¾ x ⅞-inch piece of hardwood of the appropriate length. Cut out the holes with a dado blade on a table or

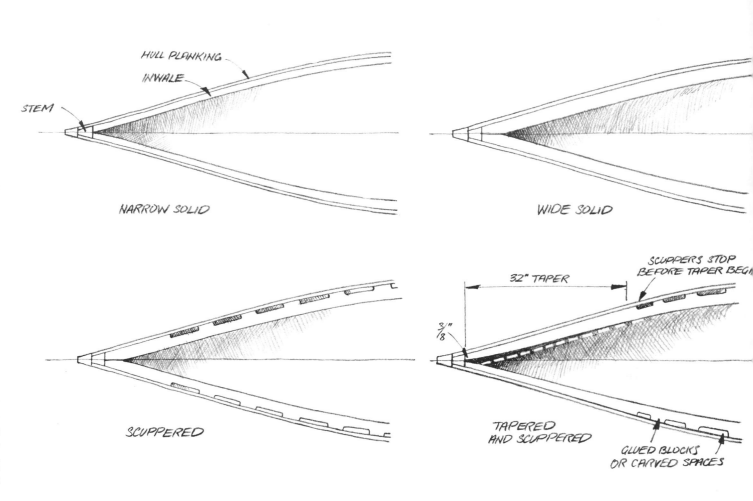

*Solid inwales, **top**, are the easiest to make, but when wide, they are too heavy, and when narrow, will not hold a seat. Tapered and/or scuppered inwales, **bottom**, are more functional and look more elegant.*

radial arm saw, a jig saw, a router with a core box veiner bit or with the edge of a large 1-to-1½-inch Forstner or saw-tooth machine bit.

Alternatively, cut blocks from ¼ x ¾-inch lumber. For an interesting visual effect, use different coloured wood or scrap planking. Using epoxy resin, glue and clamp the blocks to a ¾ x ⅝-inch piece of hardwood a few inches longer than the sheer line. When dry, remove clamps and sand off excess glue. Round the inside edges of the holes with a rasp, scraper or sandpaper.

To complement the fine, graceful lines of the canoe, the inwales may be tapered toward the stems. Starting about 32 inches from each end, shape the deck-side edge of the inwale from ⅞ inch to ⅜ inch. With tapered inwales, scuppers should be stopped before the taper begins (page 74).

Outwales

Outwales (the other half of gunwales) should be wide enough to turn aside waves but not so wide as to inhibit the paddler from reaching the water. Cut from ¾-inch lumber, they can range in width from ¾ inch to 1⅛ inches, but ⅞ inch is a workable median.

Rip the outwales from a good clear piece of hardwood (or spruce if you want to reduce weight), slightly longer than the sheer of the canoe.

To give the outwale a finer line and to reduce weight without impeding function, bevel its bottom edge so the final outside thickness is ⅝ inch (see right). Shape it in the same manner as the keel, rough cutting with the saw blade set to the angle drawn on the end of the stock and shaping the final edge with the plane and/or cabinet scraper.

For even more finesse, the outwales can be tapered toward the stems. The cut is made on the hull side if the outwale is bevelled; otherwise, it is made on the outside. Beginning 32 inches from each end, taper from the full width to ⅜ inch at the stem. Cut the line roughly on the table saw, then clean up the cut with the plane or cabinet scraper. Edges may be rounded and sanded before or after the outwale is fastened to the hull.

Machining the Decks

Decks tie the two sides of a canoe together at the stems, both structurally and aesthetically. They can be as short as a simple breasthook or extend for almost the entire length of the canoe, leaving only an oval Rob-Roy-style cockpit in the centre. The decks shown in this book cover a range of styles and are completely interchangeable.

There are almost endless variations in deck design, depending on your resources and the time and effort you want to put into that part of your boat. It is here that you can let your imagination soar and make your canoe truly distinctive.

Begin by preparing a cardboard pattern of your own design or take

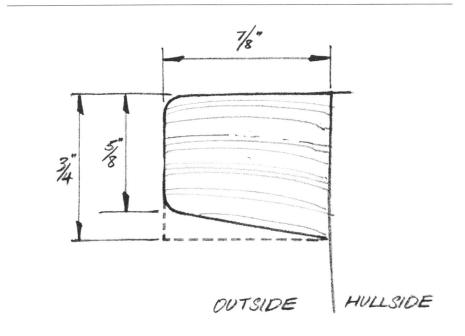

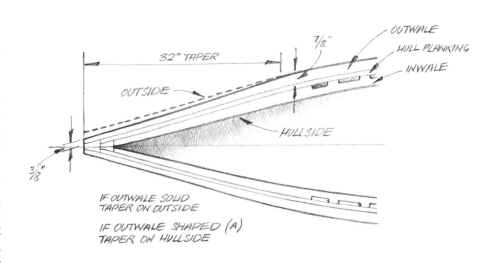

Outwales can be tapered so that all lines flow smoothly toward the ends of the canoe. To reduce weight, their bottoms can be bevelled on a table saw.

dimensions from the line drawings. When machining the decks, leave an extra ¼ inch of wood on all sides for fitting. Since they are glued to the inwales, they should end up the same thickness.

The simplest deck is shaped from a single piece of ¾-inch hardwood, though because of the deck's triangular shape, the length will be limited by the width of the board (page 77). Cut it out, and shape the front edge so it is visually pleasing and comfortably accommodates the shape of the hand, since you will probably use this as a grip to haul your canoe out of the water.

If your lumber is too narrow to make a deck of the desired length, or if you want to explore a deck's visual possibilities, you can join two boards with a spline. Keep in mind that the grain should always follow the line of the inwales, keeping the short grain on the inside where it is tied together with the spline. Arranged this way, the grain lines will converge at the stem, complementing the overall symmetry of the canoe.

Make a diagonal cut in a ¾-inch board (page 77). Flop one triangle so the acute points meet as shown. Mark which side will be the top of the deck. Set the saw blade at ⅜ inch and cut a ⅜-inch-deep by ⅛-inch-wide groove in the mating surfaces of the triangles, pressing the bottom side of each deck piece against the table to ensure that the spline grooves will line up exactly. Cut a ⅛ x ¾-inch hardwood spline the length of the deck, and dry fit

the triangles together with the spline. Set the deck on your bench, which should be protected with plastic or wax paper. Make a clamping jig by screwing 1 x 2-inch blocks along the inwale sides of the deck, fastening one to the bench with two screws, and one with a pivot screw in the centre. Remove the deck, separate the parts, and apply glue to all mating surfaces. Fit the deck together and slide it into the jig, letting the pivot block find its own angle; then clamp a block at the front to keep the deck firmly in the jig. When the glue is set, remove from the jig and shape the front edge as above.

With the basic technique of the spline joint, the design possibilities become endless. The two triangles can be separated by a straight or tapered piece of wood of contrasting colour, fastened with two splines. By putting a slight angle on the mating edges of the triangles, you can create a cambered deck that complements the curving lines of your canoe.

For interesting texture, try a bookmatch deck: Instead of cutting two triangles, cut one from a 1¾-inch board, slice it down the middle, and open it up so the grain is mirrored on both sides (page 78).

To make a deck of alternating dark and light stripes, glue together ¾-inch strips of the desired width and the length of the deck. When you have a board half the width of the deck, cut it diagonally and flop one triangle to produce central converging stripes.

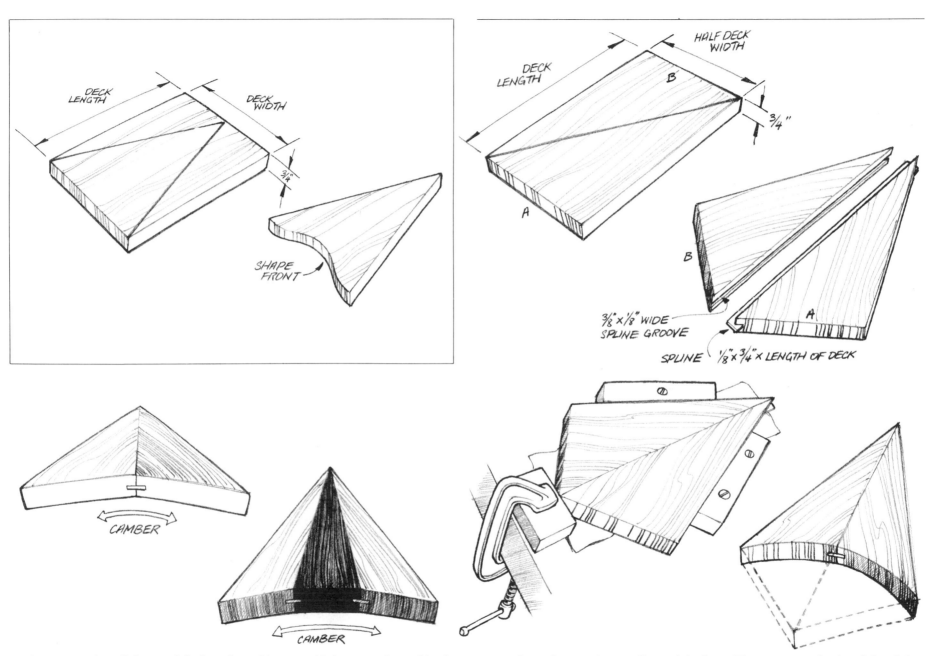

Facing page: *A well-designed deck such as this one, with its tapered panel in the centre, draws the eye toward the stem.* **This page:** *While a simple deck,* **top left**, *can be cut from one piece of wood, more elegant decks,* **top right**, *can be made with two or three pieces, using a spline to join them. The parts are glued and then left to dry in a jig,* **bottom right**. *A gentle curve, or camber,* **bottom left**, *can also be added.*

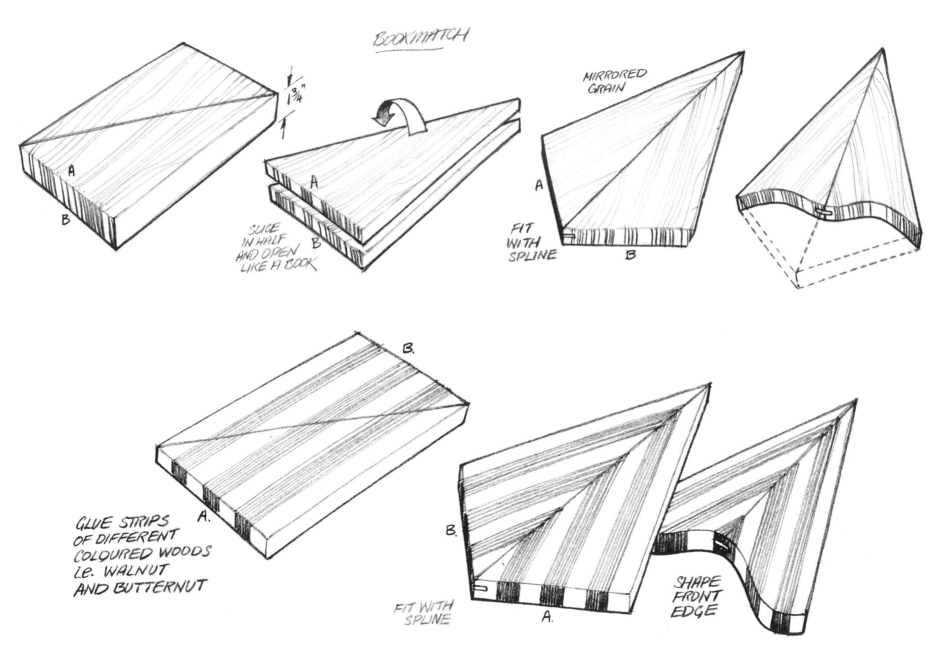

BOOKMATCH

1 3/4"

SLICE IN HALF AND OPEN LIKE A BOOK

A

B

MIRRORED GRAIN

A

B

FIT WITH SPLINE

B.

A.

GLUE STRIPS OF DIFFERENT COLOURED WOODS i.e. WALNUT AND BUTTERNUT

B.

A.

FIT WITH SPLINE

SHAPE FRONT EDGE

Top: *Bookmatch decks, cut from a thick board of highly figured wood like bird's-eye maple, feature a perfectly matched grain that radiates toward the stem of the canoe.*

Below: *Contrasting woods can be laminated into a single plank, then cut and splined together to form a dramatic arrow formation.*

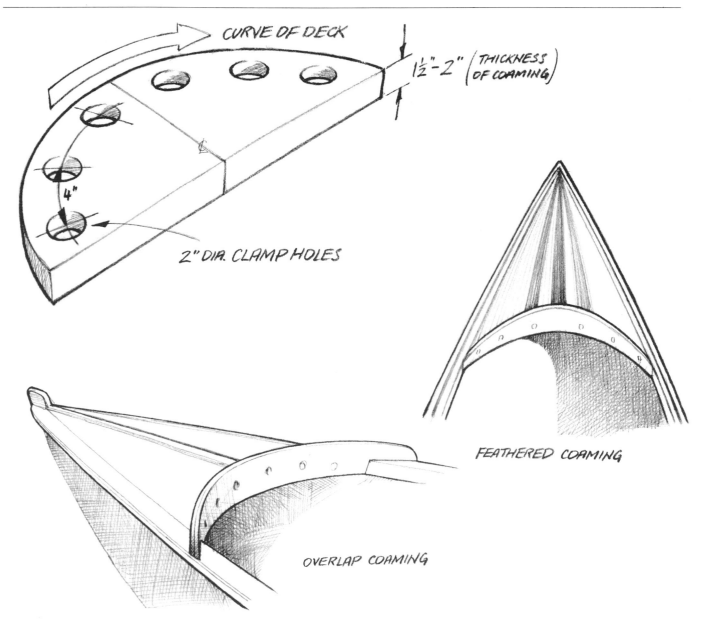

CURVE OF DECK

1½"-2" (THICKNESS OF COAMING)

4"

2" DIA. CLAMP HOLES

FEATHERED COAMING

OVERLAP COAMING

A traditional coaming can be added to decorate the deck's edge. To reproduce the exact curve of the deck, the coaming is steam-bent on a mould, **top,** *drilled to accommodate C-clamps.*

The coaming ends can be feathered into the inwales, **lower right,** *or its curving top can be half-lapped over the entire gun-wale,* **lower left.**

The type of wood you choose for your decks matters little as long as it has sufficient grain strength to hold the gunwales together. If you use a softer wood like cedar, you can tie the grain together with a coaming, a feature traditionally seen on vintage Peterborough canoes. Visually, it lends a luxurious air to your canoe, especially if highly figured, richly coloured woods are used.

The coaming will also cover the exposed grain at the front edge of the deck. As the illustrations indicate, the coaming can either feather into the inwale or extend over the gunwales (left). It is made by laminating together three 1½ x ⅛-inch strips of a good-looking hardwood that bends easily (cherry, oak or ash).

To reproduce the curve of the deck correctly, make a simple two-part mould. It must be the same thickness as the coaming and follow the line of the deck's front edge. Steam the hardwood strips (page 80), and then, with the bottom of the mould clamped securely in a bench vise, lay on the warm, damp strips and tightly clamp the top of the mould over them. After 24 hours, remove the strips to dry, waiting for another day before spreading epoxy glue on all inside surfaces. Clamp it again in the mould, but not so tightly that all the glue is squeezed out, starving the joints. Wipe the laminated joints clean, and when the glue has set, remove the coaming from the mould and sand smooth.

The coaming can also be formed on a one-piece mould (page 91) that is similar to a stem mould in that the laminations are held in place with a succession of C-clamps secured through clamp holes. (For a fuller discussion of steaming and laminating techniques, turn to page 90.)

on a one-piece mould (page 91)

Dry fit the coaming onto the deck, and screw with 1¼-inch #6 round head screws. Only after the deck is secured between the inwales is the coaming fastened permanently with glue and screws. Counterboring and plugs are options.

Machining Thwarts

Thwarts tie the canoe together in the middle, sometimes doubling as seat rests and carrying handles, so they should be strong enough to support a person's weight and comfortable to the hand and shoulder if they are to be used for short portages. Beware, though, of letting their utilitarian function spoil the appearance of your canoe. Some builders have ruined the lines of their craft by inserting heavy-duty dowelling that resembles a sausage; concentrate on making it attractive no matter how simple.

Thwarts can take any shape, and because they require little wood and their figured surfaces are highly visible, this is an excellent place to use those fancy hardwoods of your dreams.

With a little extra work, you can cut the board to a shape of your

Above left: *Coaming can also be shaped on a two-part mould. First the strips are steamed and shaped in the mould, and later, after drying, they are glued together,* **above right.** *Hardwood thwarts need not add weight if they are well designed,* **bottom.** *Notice how the shallow arch on the wide central areas is attractively complemented by the rounded narrow parts on either side of the thwart.*

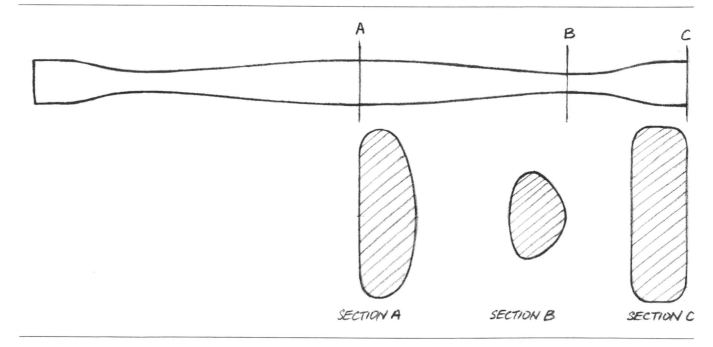

SECTION A   SECTION B   SECTION C

own design. Draw half the pattern, and repeat it for a consistent flow of lines (page 80). Round off the edges, and sand it to a fine finish.

For a more unique thwart that releases the dynamic character of the wood and comfortably takes the curve of the hand, refine the flat cutout with a spokeshave so that the widest part is thinnest and the narrow areas a little thicker, with the lines flowing smoothly between. Sculpting the thwart takes only a little extra effort, yet it will reduce weight and accentuate the grain dramatically. It should be finished by smoothing with a cabinet scraper and/or sanding with #120 grit. For a finer finish with hard grain, wet it down, then sand again with #220 grit. Apply varnish (page 134).

Machining the Seats

Like decks, seats are infinitely variable and can reflect the whims of the builder. Whatever the covering, they are all stretched over the same basic frame, constructed from ¾ x 1½-inch hardwood. The 10 x 15-inch seat frame described below not only fits most canoes but accommodates most derrieres.

Begin by laying out the frame members on the workbench. Fasten them together with two 2-inch #6 screws at each joint, predrilled, countersunk and counterbored if plugs are desired (page 130). Dismantle the frame, apply epoxy glue to all mating surfaces, then screw permanently into place.

These screws may get in the way if you are making a drilled or routed seat. In that case, join the seat frames with a simple dowel. Clamp the frame in position on the bench and drill two ¼-inch holes through both frame parts at each joint. Plane two edges of a ¼-inch dowel slightly, glue and press in place. Cut off flush. If you have the equipment and expertise, mortice and tenon or blind dowel joints are ideal.

When the joints are secure, round off the edges of the seat frame and sand with #120 grit. Finish-sand with #220 grit. Varnish with at least three coats over any exposed wood (page 134).

In choosing a covering for your seat frames, your priorities should be comfort, durability and style. Most variations are within the capabilities of amateurs, though cane and rawhide may be exceptions. Good-quality models of both types are readily available at a reasonable price (see Sources), so it might be easier to buy a seat from professionals, instead of having to spend the time to learn how to weave cane.

With seats, as with all the trim, there are two ways of approaching the machining process. On the one hand, you can hone your woodworking skills on these small projects without wasting a lot of materials, as you build up your confidence for the hull. Or, if you are a purist in matters of colour and line, you may want to wait until the hull takes shape before designing trim that will be its perfect complement.

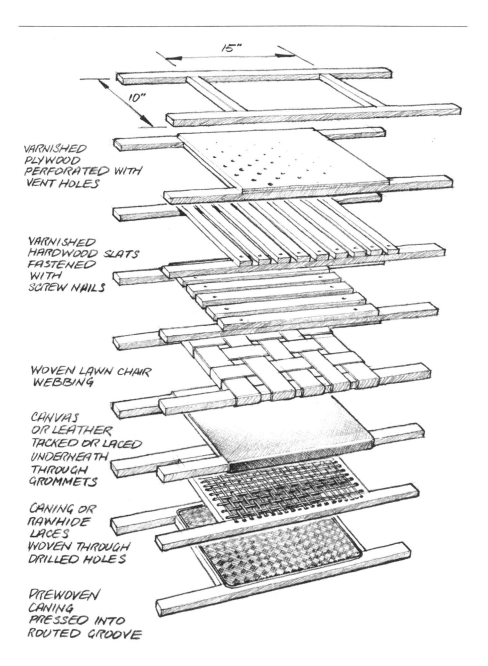

15"

10"

VARNISHED PLYWOOD PERFORATED WITH VENT HOLES

VARNISHED HARDWOOD SLATS FASTENED WITH SCREW NAILS

WOVEN LAWN CHAIR WEBBING

CANVAS OR LEATHER TACKED OR LACED UNDERNEATH THROUGH GROMMETS

CANING OR RAWHIDE LACES WOVEN THROUGH DRILLED HOLES

PREWOVEN CANING PRESSED INTO ROUTED GROOVE

A simple 10 x 15-inch hardwood seat frame is the basis for almost unlimited seat coverings, which should be chosen for their durability and comfort.

FUNCTIONAL FORM

Making the Mould

My boats and canoes have been built with as much real value in them as time and care and skill and the will to build on a quality basis could make possible.

— *Walter Dean*

To build the perfect canoe, one must have the perfect mould. To start with less than the best mould you can create is pure folly, for every imperfect curve and twist on the form will be exactly reproduced in your canoe. As a result, translating your paper plan into a working mould is a time-consuming and painstaking process that may, at first glance, hardly seem to warrant the effort involved. Certainly, if you can beg, borrow or rent the forms for a nicely shaped canoe, by all means do so. But because of the hours of effort you will put into building the hull, just be sure the mould is worth borrowing before you build on it. Do not rely on someone else's preparatory

work unless you are familiar with the canoe that last came off the mould. If it cuts through the waves like an arrow and has all the design features you need, congratulate yourself on your own good fortune, and borrow the mould before the owner changes his mind. But if the canoe paddles like a barge and looks like a watering trough, you had best rejoin the ranks of the miserable majority who must suffer the trials of assembling a mould of their own.

Actually, while it is perhaps the most exacting part of your project, building the mould is not really difficult and can actually become quite exhilarating as you gradually see the shape of things to come.

MAKING THE MOULD

Tools:

  clamps
  coping saw
  square
  pen
  scissors
  jig saw

Materials:

  two 4 x 8-foot sheets particle
    board
  carbon paper
  ¾-inch finishing nails
  masking tape

The task at hand is to take the body plan and translate its station lines into the wooden forms that will allow you to duplicate the ex-

act shape and dimensions of your canoe. But before using the station lines from your full-size grid paper to make a mould, you must have a suitable sheet of wood. I normally use particle board, cutting the 4 x 8-foot sheets into two 2 x 8-foot panels. Because all but the midpoint station must be duplicated on a symmetrical canoe in order to get both a front and back to the canoe, you will make two station moulds at a time, laying one sheet atop another so that you can cut exact duplicates of the matching stations.

Presumably, the factory can cut straighter than we can, so line up the uncut edges of the sheets, and clamp them together. Line up the

baseline of the plan with the uncut edge, and mark the position of the centreline on the board. Remove the plan, and using a square, draw the centreline perpendicular to the uncut edge. *Make sure it is dead on.* This will be your primary guide when setting up the moulds.

Cut two small (¼-inch) windows out of the plan near the top and bottom of the centreline. Lay the plan on the board, using the windows to match up the centrelines, and secure the pattern with masking tape.

Slide carbon paper face down under the plan, and pressing firmly with a ballpoint pen, trace the shape as smoothly and accurately as possible. If your paper is transparent, the markings will still be visible when you flip it to draw the other half of the mould. If it is opaque, put a second layer of carbon paper face up under the plan, so that as the first half of the mould is traced, the image is transferred both to the board and to the back side of the plan. Also, with opaque paper, remember to trace the centreline so it will be visible on the plan's back side.

Flip the plan over, line up the centreline through the windows, tape in place, and then use carbon paper to trace the other half of this station. Then remove the plan and inscribe the mould with the station number.

Reproduce all the contours in this manner except for the stem. Since the plan is *not* flipped, the stem will look like half a mould.

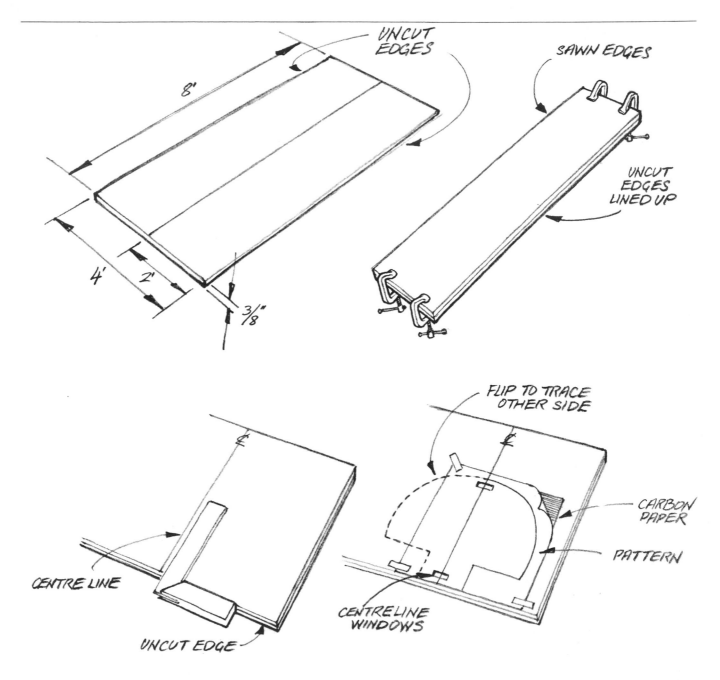

Transferring the pattern to plywood

When the outlines of all moulds are traced, fasten the duplicates together, one atop its twin, with two or three ¾-inch finishing nails inside each station. This will keep the two pieces lined up as you cut around the outline.

Using a sabre saw, band saw or electric jig saw, cut out the first mould, being careful to stay on the line. If the saw wanders outside the line, the edge can be dressed, but if it wanders inside, the mould will be misshapen. Make a shallow sawcut (⅛-inch) in the top and bottom of the centreline, through both thicknesses. This will be a vital reference for lining up the stations on the strongback.

Remove the nails and separate the twin moulds, marking the station number on the duplicate, and then, using the sawcuts, draw a centreline on the three sides that do not yet have one.

Repeat this procedure with each pattern piece except the stem moulds. Before the stem moulds are separated, cut 2-inch holes spaced at 4-inch centres, one inch from the edge. When it is laminated, the stem will be clamped through these holes, so be sure they accommodate your clamps.

BUILDING THE STRONGBACK

Tools:

taut line	crosscut saw
pencil	hammer
square	clamps
plane	drill
	screwdriver

Materials:

two 2 x 10-inch planks
two 2 x 10 x 32-inch planks (legs)
four corner blocks
2 x 4 x 24-inch planks (feet)
1½-inch #6 flathead screws

The strongback is the backbone that supports the mould sections and controls the finished shape of the canoe and, as such, must be as perfect as possible, level in all directions, straight and solid.

There are as many styles of strongbacks as there are builders, but the T-beam is one of the most stable and one of the easiest to build. Select two clear, straight 2 x 10-inch softwood planks as long as the stem-to-stem dimensions of the canoe. A slight warp is acceptable but a twist is not, however minor. Good-quality, fully dried used lumber is preferable to fresh green planks that tend to corkscrew, as one group of eager young boatbuilders found out. Having used green lumber in their strongback, they set up the moulds and planked half the hull within days. But after a weekend away, they returned to find that the strongback had twisted the hull into an S-curve. They were forced to dismantle the hull and mould and start over.

To build the T-beam, the vertical "spine" is prepared first, planed straight and square to support the horizontal "plate" (page 86). Lay the straightest of the two planks face down. Stretch a taut line tightly along one edge. If the line runs

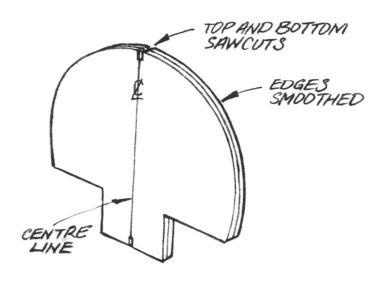

A station mould

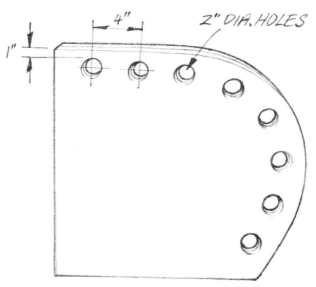

A stem mould

parallel to the edge for the full length, you are in luck. If not, this edge must be straightened to support the plate squarely. Mark the board with a pencil point every couple of feet along the line, then join the dots with a straight edge. Chalk lines, though fine for rough carpentry, are not precise enough for canoe construction.

The next step is to transfer the line to the opposite side of the plank. Using a square for accuracy, continue the line across both ends of the board. With the plank turned over, stretch a taut line between the two end points, and mark this second face with a pencil as you did the first. With the dots connected, you will have matching parallel lines on both faces.

Now, with your longest plane, dress the edge of the board down to these lines. Work at it until the edge is perfectly square with the face of the plank. Cut the spine to length, slightly shorter than the plate to accommodate the plate's pointed ends.

The second long plank is the plate on which the moulds are fastened. Like the spine, it should be as straight as possible, for if there is a hump in the plate, there will be a hump in your hull.

On the underside of the plate, draw guidelines the same width as the spine's planed edge so the T-beam and the plate can be squarely fastened together. To do this, mark the centreline of the plate, then measure half the width of the spine edge on either side. Using a taut

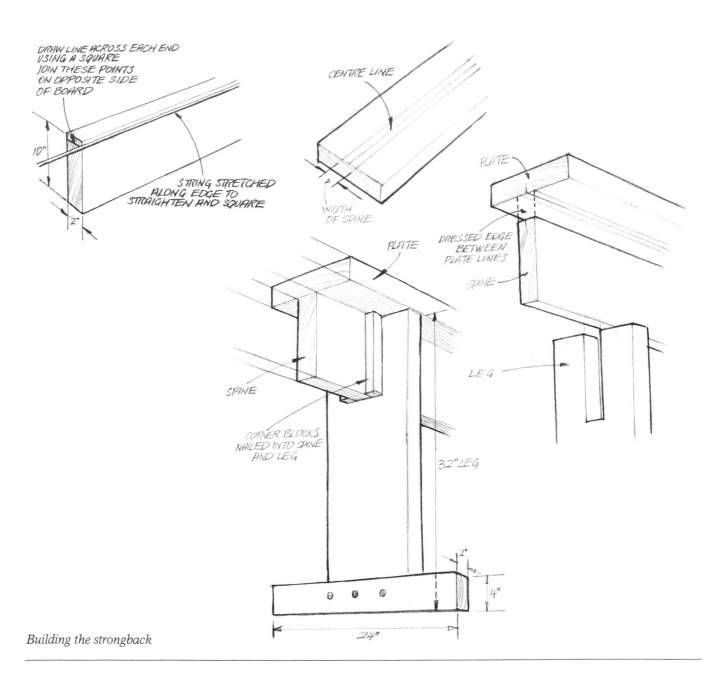

Building the strongback

line, connect the guidelines.

Set the spine on edge, and lay the plate on top so that the spine's planed edge fits precisely between the guidelines on the plate (page 86). Nail the plate to the spine using 3½-inch common or spiral nails at 1-foot intervals, or for greater control and accuracy and easier dismantling, screw down the plate with 3-inch #8 screws.

Make a support stand for this T-beam by cutting two 2 x 10-inch legs, long enough to put the strongback at a comfortable working level (32 inches will suit builders of average height). Mark the centre of the cut edge, then scribe a notch that fits exactly the dimension of the spine (page 86). Saw down each side of the notch, drill to perforate just above the bottom line, and chisel out the notch. If the spine sits snugly in the notches at the top of each leg, the T-beam will be stabilized and less prone to twisting.

Temporarily clamp a 2 x 4 x 24-inch foot to the bottom of each leg. Set up the strongback in its canoe-building position, lowering the T-beam into the leg notches, spacing the legs two to three feet from each end of the plate. Secure each leg at right angles to the plate by nailing four small softwood corner blocks into both the spine and leg, or pre-drill and fasten with 1½-inch #6 flathead screws. Nail or screw the feet to the legs so the plate is perfectly level (although the feet won't be if the floor isn't level). Finally, eliminate all wiggles by nailing the feet to the floor or weighting them down with cement blocks.

If you have been accurate at every stage, your finished strongback will be level and square.

SETTING UP THE MOULD

Tools:

 taut line
 straight edge
 pencil
 set square
 drill
 countersink bit
 clamp

Materials:

 1½ x 1½ x 9½ inch station
  blocks
 2-inch #8 screws
 1-inch #6 screws
 two ¾-inch square corner blocks
 paraffin

With all this picky, monotonous work, you may not feel much like a boatbuilder. But as you set up the mould, prepare for a thrill as the first skeletal image of your canoe emerges. Even after many years of boatbuilding, it is impossible not to feel a surge of excitement at setting up a new mould.

To begin, use a taut line to rule a line down the centre of the plate, pressing hard enough to dent the surface of the wood with a strong dark impression. This is the centreline.

With a square, draw a line perpendicular to the centreline at its midpoint. This is the midsection

When attaching a mould to the strongback, screw one side to its station block, then check that the centreline is vertical before fastening the other side. Shimming may be necessary.

station and the midsection mould will be fastened directly over it. Measuring from this point, draw all the station lines at equal intervals as specified. The rest of the moulds will be fastened on the side of the station line closest to the centre.

Cut a block 1½ x 1½ x 9½ inches for each station. At the centreline, position the block half the mould thickness to one side of the line. Drill the block with a countersink bit, and fasten to the strongback with two 2-inch #8 screws.

Designate the bow end of the plate, which, if the stems are symmetrical, will be an arbitrary decision. Moving toward the bow, fasten a block on the bow side of each station line until you reach the last. Cut a block in two, and fasten half on either side of the baseline at a 90-degree angle to the last station, leaving a space the thickness of the stem mould between them, as shown at right.

Fasten blocks at the station lines from the midsection to the stern, screwing them on the stern side of each station line. When you reach the stern, set out two blocks on either side of the baseline for the stern stem, as you did at the bow.

Finally, double-check that all blocks are at right angles to the plate and to the baseline.

In setting up the actual mould, the stem sections are positioned first. They consist of two parts: the stem mould and the station mould that is perpendicular to it at bow and stern.

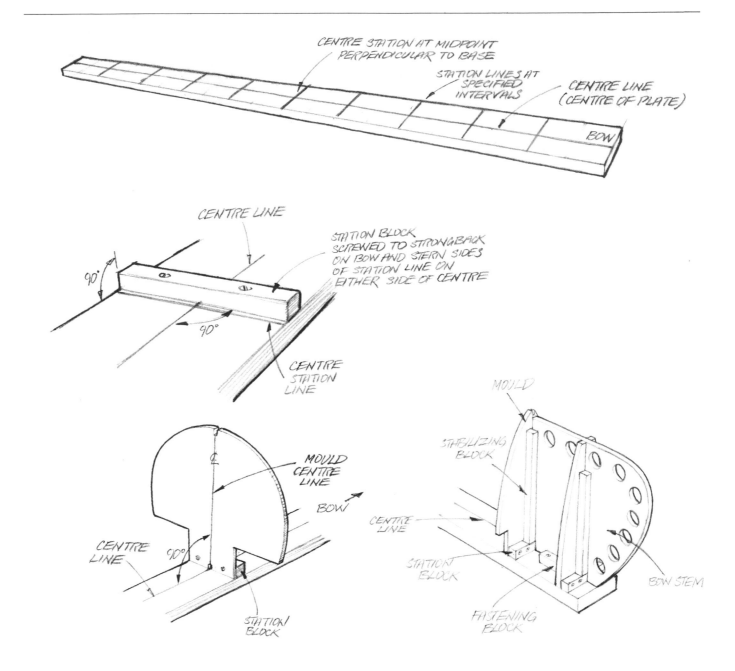

Attaching the moulds to the strongback

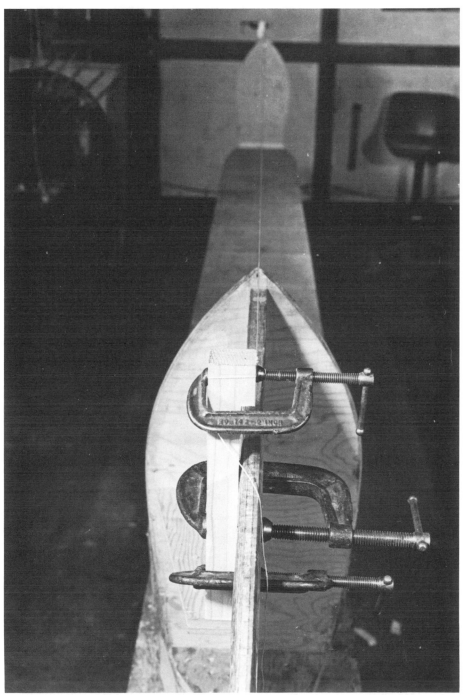

Above, *after the stem moulds are set up perfectly plumb, stretch a taut line between them. Clamp the string — do not tie it — so that it runs directly down the centreline one inch above the highest mould section. When added to the strongback, each station mould's centreline notch,* **right**, *should fall directly under the line.*

to the stems.

Beginning at the bow, clamp the second last station mould section to its block, positioning the bottom notch directly over the centreline. Check with a level to make sure the mould centreline is plumb, then fasten by screwing 1-inch #6 screws through the mould into the block. The top may be wobbly, but do not worry about it yet.

Centre the bow stem mould on the baseline between the blocks. Screw the mould into a fastening block attached to the strongback. Line up the stem mould with the centreline of the bow mould, tying the two together with a ¾-inch-square stabilizing block almost the height of the moulds. Double-check for plumbness (page 89). Then, to set up the last station, cut it in half (deducting the thickness of the stem mould), and fasten it with a stabilizing block on either side of the stem mould. Set up the stern section in the same way.

As a reference point for elevation and straightness, stretch a taut line between the bow and the stern. Clamp, don't tie, the string to a block secured to each stem section. Drawn tight, it must be centred over the top notches of the bow and stern moulds and raised enough to clear the highest mould.

Set up the rest of the moulds, on the midsection side of their blocks, positioning the bottom notch over the baseline and the top notch under the taut line. As you fasten each to its station block, check that the mould centreline is plumb, and

shim it if necessary.

When all the moulds are fastened in place, cut the strongback flush with the stems, and angle it back towards the centre.

Finally, remove the taut line and sight down the top notches. This is the line that is going to slice through waves, so be sure it is perfectly straight.

LAMINATING THE STEMS

Tools:

steaming/soaking equipment
clamps   spokeshave
block plane   batten

Materials:

six or twelve ¼ x ¾ x 40 to
    50-inch hardwood strips
string
plastic sheet   epoxy solvent
epoxy glue   sandpaper #120
four 1½ x 1½ x ¾-inch stem
    blocks

Safety:

gloves   barrier cream

The stems, together with the keel and gunwales, are a vital link in the skeleton of a canoe. They absorb and distribute impacts to the bow. Inside stems support the ends of the strips, improving control during planking. Outside stems originally sealed the exposed end-grain of cedar planking, but with epoxy construction, they serve primarily to add a traditional finishing touch to the canoe.

Steam-bending a single piece of wood into a stem requires special equipment and exerts considerable

tension and compression on the wood fibres. A simpler solution that reduces fibre stress is to laminate several thin strips which have been easily bent in a makeshift steam box.

For each stem, select three strips of clear, straight-grained hardwood ¼ x ¾ x 40 or 50 inches long. (Lengths vary with canoe design but will generally be a couple of inches longer than the curve of the stem mould itself.) These strips are bent wet over the stem mould, allowed to dry, then glued together and shaped. Outside stems must be steam-bent at the same time as the inside stems so they will fit snugly over top.

The strips can be bent by soaking them overnight in a bathtub of hot water. In the morning, drain the tub, refill it with the hottest water possible, and soak the strips for another half-hour before bending. The hotter and wetter the wood, the more flexible it becomes and the less prone it is to breaking.

For quicker wetting and faster drying, use a makeshift steam box (page 91). Insert the strips in a metal, plastic or cardboard tube slightly longer than the wood. Plug the top tightly, and wrap the bottom with a loose-weave cloth. Fill an electric kettle with water, and set the tube over the spout. Bring the water to a boil, and steam for 30 to 45 minutes until the wood is very flexible.

Before soaking or steaming the strips, designate how they will be stacked, with the clearest, straight-

est grain on the outside, potential defects in the centre. Once you remove them from the heat, you will not have any time for such weighty decisions.

I usually bend the stems by myself with the stem mould clamped in the bench vise, but for the novice, it is easier to bend them at the strongback with the help of an extra pair of hands. Remove the strips from the steam box, stack them in order, and position them on top of the stem mould, butting them squarely up to the bow section. While one person holds and bends the strips, the other should clamp the laminations securely at the first hole. Be careful not to distort or compress the wet wood. Continue around the stem curve, bending and clamping. Move slowly enough so that the outer strip has time to stretch but briskly enough to prevent the wood from cooling and stiffening. Six clamps should keep the laminated strips smooth as they dry.

After 24 hours, remove the strips from the mould, tie a taut string from one end of each stem bundle to the other, and hang to dry (page 92). Steam-bent strips will need only 24 hours; water-bent should hang for two to three days.

When the strips are ready to glue, protect your floor or workbench with a sheet of plastic, and lay out the inside stem pieces in order. Spread an even coat of epoxy glue on each of the four inside surfaces, and press together. Clamp the laminated stem firmly to the

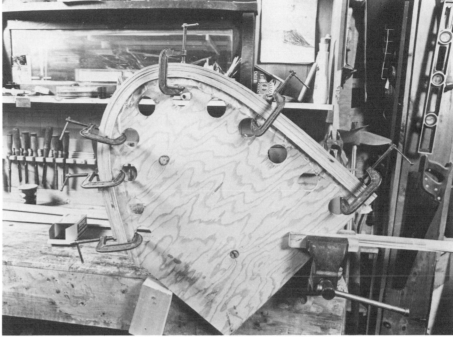

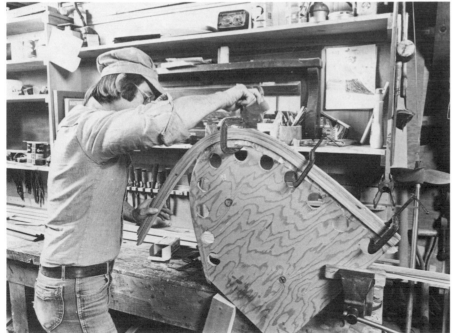

Top left: *An electric kettle and a length of cardboard tubing make an excellent steam box. Slip the wood strips into the tube and set over a boiling kettle, plugging the top and base of the tube. After 30 to 45 minutes, the strips should be hot, wet and pliable.*
Bottom left: *Although you can shape your stems right on the stem mould itself, I use a mould clamped in a bench vise. Each stem needs three strips butted evenly at their keel end. It is often easier bending and clamping the strips with the help of another person.* **Above:** *Leave the clamped strips on the mould for 24 hours.*

bow stem mould. Some glue will ooze out the side, but do not clamp so tightly that all the glue squeezes out, starving the joint. Scrape off excess glue with a putty knife, and wipe the joints clean. If there is an outside stem, glue it together, and clamp it onto the mould at the same time as the inside stem. Some glue may smear over the edges, but when dry, just sand it off, and the two stems will pop apart.

When thoroughly set, remove the stem from the mould, and sand off any excess glue. If you wish, round off the end section of the inside stem at the keel line, where it will be visible inside the boat, as shown at right.

For the planking to lay flat, this chunky square stem has to be shaped with a rolling bevel from the sheer-line to the keel-line (page 93). Draw a centreline down the leading edge of the inside stem as a reference point. The stem must be dressed to within 1/16 inch on either side of this line. (Note: If you will be adding an outside stem, leave the leading edge of the inside stem a little wider.)

Clamp the stem back on the mould, and shape with a block plane and spokeshave. To get the correct bevel at any given point, tack a batten (a 6-to-8-foot cedar strip) along the anticipated angle of planking, and curve it around to meet the stem. Plane down that side of the stem until the batten lies flat. Work your way up from the sheer-line to the keel a few inches at a time, shaping both sides of the

stem evenly. This is painstaking work, but it will save you a great deal of time and frustration later. With the bevels perfected at this stage, the hull planking will proceed quickly and smoothly.

With such a fine leading edge, the clamps can slip or crush the tapered stem; to prevent this, cut a wedge out of a 1½ x 1½ x ¾-inch block, and slip it over the stem edge before reclamping (page 93). Three or four clamps per stem should be sufficient.

FAIRING THE MOULD

Tools:

 level
 staple gun
 block plane/spokeshave
 sanding block
 rasp

Materials:

 batten
 staples

Although at this point it is natural to become anxious to begin planking the hull, it pays to take a few extra moments to check the fairness of the curves. You will notice that the moulds are still a little wiggly at the top. Stabilize them vertically by fixing one end of a long strip of planking under the first clamp that holds the bow stem to the mould. Stretch this batten along the keel line and clamp it at the stern stem. Starting at the stern section and working forward, use a level to plumb each mould,

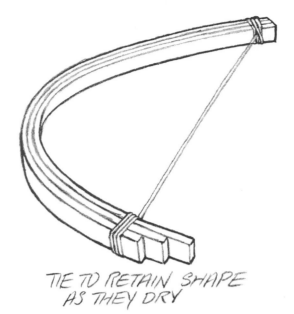

TIE TO RETAIN SHAPE AS THEY DRY

Top: *After they are removed from the mould, tie the stems and let dry for 24 hours.*
Bottom: *Inside a finished canoe, the stem adds a pleasing touch, as beautiful as it is necessary.*

then staple through the batten into the top of the mould.

With your moulds perfectly stable in all directions, you can check the fairness of the curves. Careful tracing and cutting should have reduced this stage to a pleasant formality.

Bend an 8-foot strip of planking around the moulds at the sheerline. Slowly work up to the keel along the anticipated line of planking, moving 5 inches at a time. The plank should just touch the edge of each mould. Irregularities under ⅛ inch can be tolerated on the sides and bottom, since they will spring back when the hull is taken off the mould. On hard curves, such as the turn of the bilge, accuracy should be within 1/32 inch. Shave down high spots with a plane, spokeshave, sanding block or rasp. Be careful not to remove too much. If there is a serious dip in the mould, you can glue in a piece of wood shaped to fit.

This may seem like a tedious and unnecessary step, but it will produce the smoothest lines possible in your canoe. Ultimately, you have to live with the bumps and hollows, so fair the mould to your own standard of perfection.

Now, pull up your moaning chair, and take a good long look at the skeleton of your canoe. One of the hardest and least fulfilling parts is over. On the foundation of this work, your canoe will quickly take shape. Savour the anticipation a little longer — you are only hours away from a wooden hull.

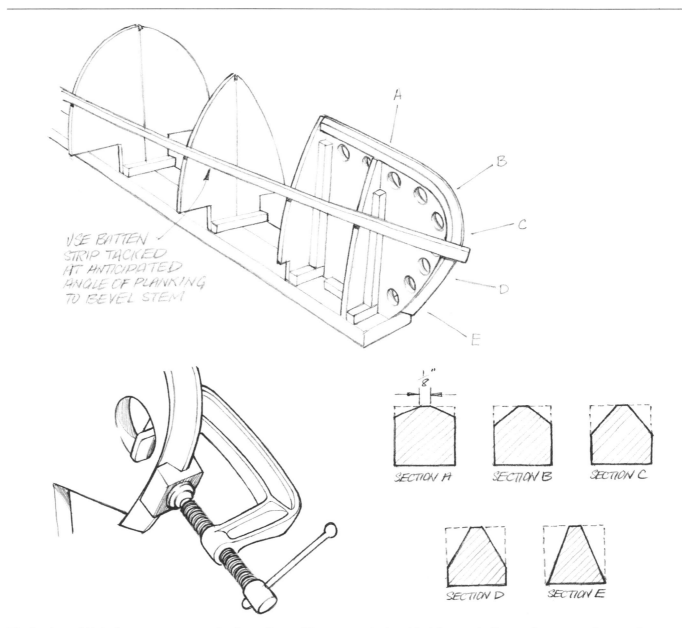

USE BATTEN STRIP TACKED AT ANTICIPATED ANGLE OF PLANKING TO BEVEL STEM

SECTION A   SECTION B   SECTION C

SECTION D   SECTION E

The laminated ¾-inch square stem must be shaped in a rolling bevel so that each plank will lie flat against it. The stem's leading edge must be ⅛-inch wide down the centre, but its shaped sides will range from a deep vee (at point E) to a shallow cut (point A). A batten indicates the appropriate angles to cut. Since the leading edge will be delicate, protect it with small blocks when clamping it in place.

THE STRIPPER'S ART

Building the Hull

The canoe implies a long antiquity in which its manufacture has been gradually perfected. It will, ere long, perhaps, be ranked among the lost arts.

— *Henry David Thoreau*

A Pacific Ocean hurricane may not be in your immediate plans, but it is reassuring to know that your canoe will be tough enough to survive that kind of abuse. In 1977, Canadians Dennis Bilodeau and Jerry LaChapelle paddled a 19-foot Wanicott woodstrip/epoxy canoe from San Francisco to Panama, in the first leg of a planned circumnavigation of North and South America. Off the coast of El Salvador, they were caught in a hurricane, standard fare for an ocean liner perhaps, but with 40-mile-per-hour winds gouging 20-foot troughs in the waves, it proved a real test for their canoe. With 1,000 pounds of gear and its occupants strapped inside, the canoe turned end over end in a situation that Bilodeau claims would have torn other canoes to pieces. Incredibly, at least for those unfamiliar with woodstrip/epoxy construction, the canoe (and paddlers) survived unscathed.

This canoe's amazing strength and beauty come from the monocoque construction of the hull. Fused together in three stages, it has a core of ¼-inch-thick strips of wood glued together on top of the series of moulds that provide its shape. These wooden strips are then draped in fibreglass, effectively sandwiched inside and out by the lightweight cloth and three coats of epoxy to give it added strength and rigidity. Even in the face of popular fibreglass and aluminum canoes, the monocoque hull is one of the toughest and most beautiful to be found, a careful blend of traditional woodstrip boat-building techniques and 20th-century technology. And as you are about to discover, building the hull is a straightforward task, easily handled in about two weeks of evenings and weekends.

PLANKING THE HULL

Tools:

staple gun	roller
level	chisel
coping saw	pencil
glue syringe	block plane
brush	taut line

dividers
rags
homemade mitre box

Materials:

paraffin
planking
staples
glue
glue solvent
two screws

Safety:

ventilation
gloves

Your wood strips have been cut from at least three different boards, and there will be surprising colour variations among the

three different bundles of strips. Because one board may have had a reddish tone, while the others were pink and tan, an indiscriminate builder who does not mix and match his planking could end up with a canoe that has large sections of hull which are all one colour or another. Builders who overlook the colour variation not only pass up a real potential for beauty, but they often detract from the good lines of their boats, with hideous blotches of red, brown and pink. At the very least, shuffle the strips a bit so the planking will be applied in random hues, colour-balanced on each side. With a little more forethought, you can use the varying tones and textures to good effect in the hull design, adding dark accent stripes just above the waterline or below the gunwales. When dark and light strips are alternated, the overturned hull resembles an enormous, elongated bull's-eye. The possibilities are almost endless.

Before starting to plank, rub the mould edges thoroughly with paraffin. This prevents the glue from sticking and will make the hull easy to lift off the moulds. Planking begins at the sheer-line and proceeds evenly up both sides, a few strips at a time, so the stems are not forced out of line. To establish the sheer plank, staple the middle of a full-length strip (keeping the concave cove-side up) to the bottom edge of the centre mould, then bend and staple it along the bottom edge of all moulds up to the stems.

The staples are merely temporary and will be removed once the hull is glued and ready to be covered. If the bow rises too sharply for the sheer plank to follow comfortably, let the plank follow the sheer-line through midships and arc naturally to the stem (page 97). The space between the sheer plank and the actual sheer-line can be filled in later with shorter planks. This was the solution for the sharply curving sheer on the original cedarstrips of the Peterborough Canoe Company. When the first plank is in place, stand at the stem and eyeball the curve: the sheer plank should flow smoothly from mould to mould without any waves. (If a plank sits too high or low on a station, pull the staple and set it straight. It is important to get the first plank straight as it is the foundation of your strips.) If the plank lies evenly, cut it off flush with the stems at right angles to the keel-line (page 97). Do not, however, attach it to the stem yet.

Tack a sheer plank to the opposite side of the centre mould, and level across to the first plank so the two sides are even (page 98). Staple this second sheer plank so it sits flush with the bottom of each mould, keeping it level with the other side. Once again, check it for fairness when finished, and cut it to length. Then glue and staple both sheer planks to the stems.

Working on one side, squeeze a bead of glue into the cove of the sheer plank and press the next

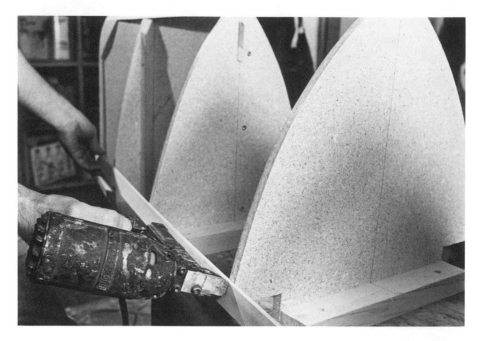

Top: *Staple the sheer plank along the bottom edge of each mould, starting at the centre and working towards the stems.* **Bottom:** *The trough of a bead-and-cove plank eases the application of glue.*

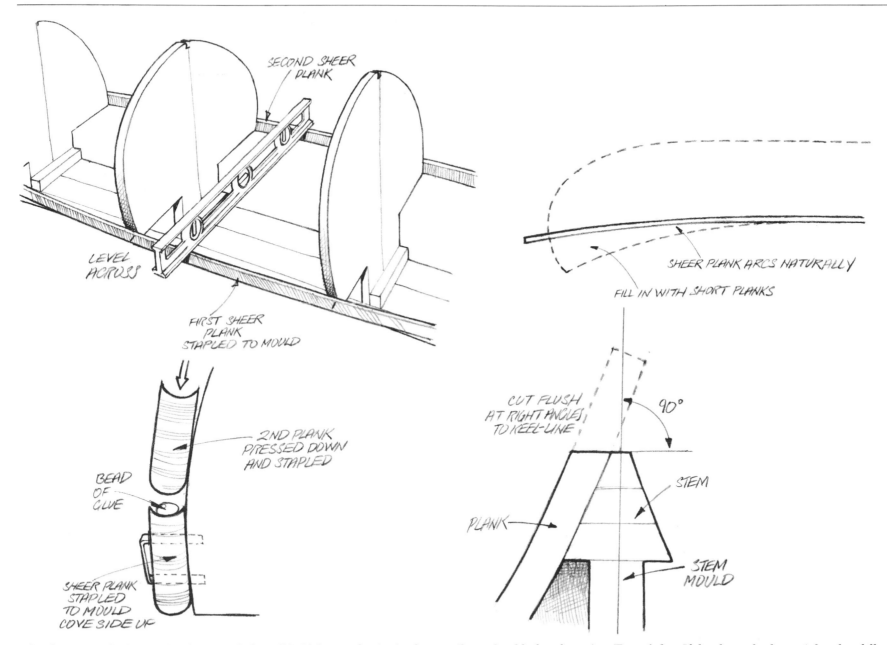

SECOND SHEER PLANK

LEVEL ACROSS

FIRST SHEER PLANK STAPLED TO MOULD

SHEER PLANK ARCS NATURALLY

FILL IN WITH SHORT PLANKS

2ND PLANK PRESSED DOWN AND STAPLED

BEAD OF GLUE

SHEER PLANK STAPLED TO MOULD COVE SIDE UP

CUT FLUSH AT RIGHT ANGLES TO KEEL-LINE

90°

STEM

PLANK

STEM MOULD

When laying up planks, staples, **bottom left**, will hold the wood strips in place until the glue dries. **Top left:** To ensure that both sides of the hull are even, staple the first sheer plank to the mould, and then check the position of the second sheer plank with a level before fastening. **Top right:** If the sheer plank won't bend to follow the rise of a stem, let it arc naturally, and fill in with short planks. At the stems, **bottom right**, cut each plank flush to the inside stem at right angles to the keel-line.

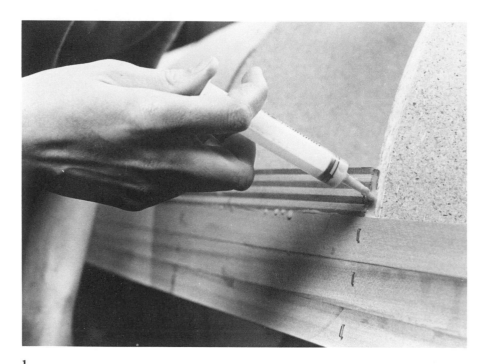

1.

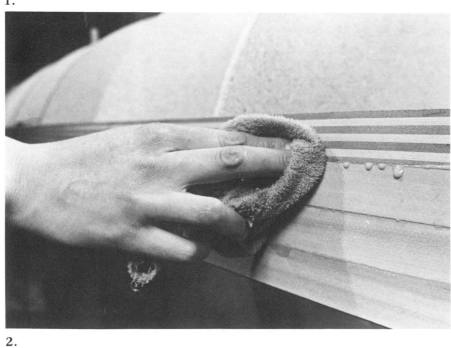

2.

3.

4.

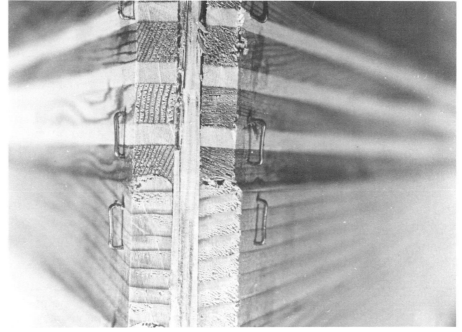

6.

1. *If a wood strip does not run the full length of the hull, join two shorter lengths with a butt joint at a station mould.* 2. *Clean up glue oozing out between the strips as soon as it appears and save hours of sanding later.* 3. *If the staples line up on the hull, the pinholes they leave behind will be less obtrusive. Note the extra staples tying planks together around the hard curve of the bilge area.* 4. *Glue short planks down to the sheer-line on canoe models that have a high recurve at either end (as in illustration on previous page).* 5. *Once the sheer-line has been filled in on one side, trim the plank ends flush with the inside stem before filling in the sheer on the opposite side.* 6. *Properly trimmed, the bow and stern's leading edge is a consistent width, with the inside stem sandwiched between the planks.*

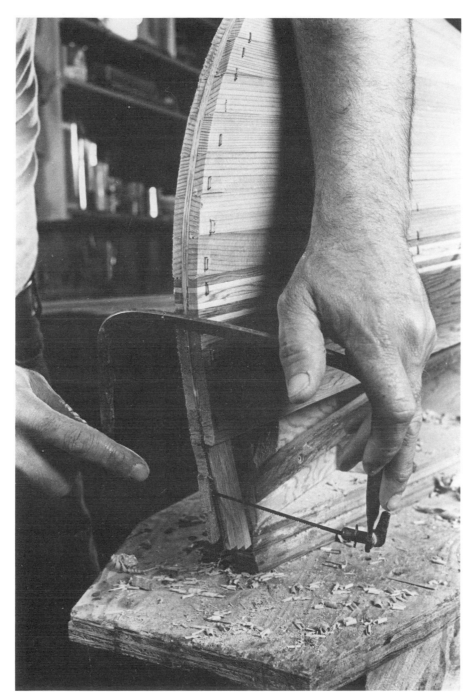

5.

plank into it (page 97). (With square-edge or shiplap planking, roll or brush the glue on the bottom edge of the *next* plank.) Beginners usually use too much glue, so be sure to put just enough on the plank edge to bond the joint. Only a small bead of glue should squeeze out when the two strips are stapled together. Wipe it off, inside and out, as you go along. Applying the right amount of glue is a knack that develops as you get comfortable with the process. But it is important. One Ohio builder lamented that he could have saved 50 hours of building time by keeping the glue under control.

Continue up the hull, stapling each plank flat against the mould at every station (or tapping in 1-inch finishing nails, leaving ⅛ inch exposed). I always line up the staples on the moulds so the pinholes that are left behind become an integral part of the canoe design, much like the copper nailheads of cedarstrip canoes.

Work at keeping the plank edges in line. This will save you a lot of sanding and filling when you fair the hull. With square-edge or shiplap planking, shoot extra staples between stations if necessary, one leg in each plank, to stitch them together. For better tying power, angle the gun as you drive in the staple (page 96). Don't use any more staples than necessary, or the hull will look like a colander when they are pulled.

Watch how the planks are landing on the shaped edge of the stem.

If necessary, dress the stem edge to make each plank lie flat before gluing and stapling. When you have a few planks fastened to one side of the hull, carefully trim the ends at each stem with a coping saw before starting to plank the other side (page 99). It is important to fasten a few planks at a time on either side of the hull so the stems remain plumb. Remove the stem clamps as you reach them.

The first few planks should run the full length of the canoe, but you may eventually have to use some shorter strips. Join them on the hull with a simple, well-glued butt joint over a mould station (page 98). Stagger the joints to avoid a structural and visual weak point at any one station.

At the bilge curve of the canoe, the planking will want to pull apart. For maximum holding strength here, shoot two staples through the plank into the mould, one to stitch the plank to the one below and one to hold the top edge of the plank tight against the mould. Be especially diligent in the bow and stern quarters at about the 4-inch waterline, where the planking is forced into a compound bend. If you need even greater holding power, use small finishing nails driven in and set halfway into the wood with a punch. If the compound bends are too great, however, you will have to add tapered "cheater" planks, about 2 feet long, fastened full-width at the stems and tapered back toward the middle (see right).

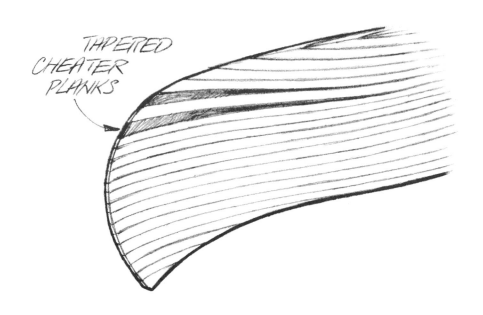

TAPERED CHEATER PLANKS

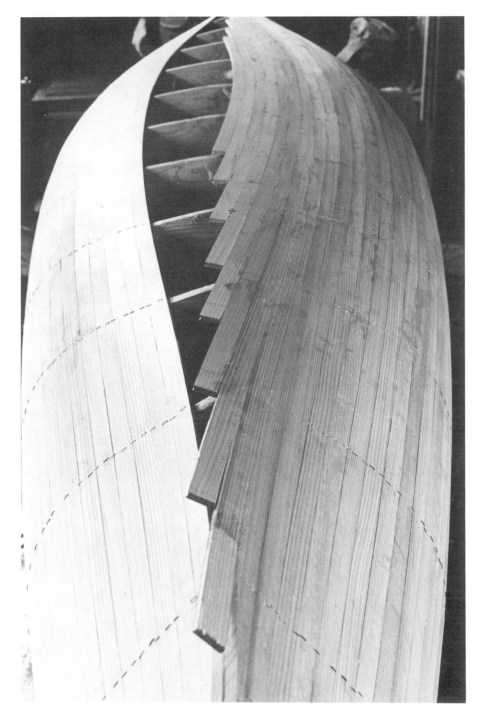

Top left: *Tapered cheater planks fill in at the compound bends that will not accommodate full-length wood strips.* **Bottom left:** *A screw through the bow and stern moulds into the stem ends will hold the stems securely once the keel batten is removed.* **Left:** *Continue planking up one side only once you have covered the stems, extending the strips over the keel-line.* **Above:** *Once the glue is firmly set, stretch a taut line from stem to stem, and draw a centreline down the keel.*

Left: *Starting in the middle of the hull and working toward the stem, chisel off the ends of the planks extending over the centreline.* **Above:** *Use a razor-sharp chisel against the grain of the planking so that the wood does not rip.* **Right:** *Smooth the centreline edge perfectly straight with a small block plane.* **Bottom right:** *To fit the final planks in the opposite side of the hull, extend the wood strip's end over the centreline, and mark the angle with a pencil. Then put the strip into a mitre box/clamping jig,* **top right**, *to hold it steady while chiselling to shape.*

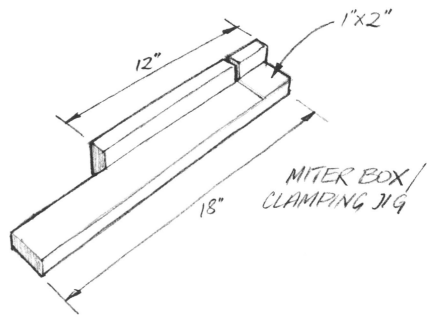

1.

3.

2.

1. *Holding the plank in a jig, chisel it to shape.* **2.** *Once the first angled end fits into the gap, draw a benchmark about a foot along the strip so that when the other end is shaped, the benchmarks can be lined up,* **3,** *and the plank glued into place.* **4.** *Remove the top cove edge from the second-last strip before it is glued into place, as the final strip will not be able to fit in between the cove edges if both are left on.* **5.** *Determine the shape of the last strip by measuring the hull's gap every one inch and transferring the points to the wood strip.* **6.** *After planing the final strip to shape, it should slip perfectly into place.*

4.

5.

6.

These will relieve the tension of the long planks and are virtually invisible.

(On these curves, only the inside edges of square-edge planking will meet, creating wide gaps on the outside. For a tight fit and for sufficient gluing surface, the inside edge of each strip will have to be bevelled.)

Continue planking up to the top of the stems. At this point, you will have to remove the last of the stem mould clamps, making the stems a bit wiggly. Secure them by running a screw through the bow and stern mould sections just barely into the stems (page 100). Remember to remove these before taking the hull off the mould.

When the planking on both sides is running almost parallel with the tops of the stems, remove the keel batten and continue planking one side only, letting the plank ends extend past the keel-line at random. Planking the side opposite your workbench is most convenient.

Let the glue cure (about 12 hours at room temperature), then draw a centreline down the keel-line. Starting in the middle and working towards the stems, cut the strips off to the line, chiselling against the grain. Smooth the edge with a block plane.

Fitting the rest of the planks into the remaining half-oval takes patience and precision. Lay the first plank in position, with the plank's excess end extending over the centreline. Mark the cut on one side and clamp it to a mitre box/clamping jig at the workbench (page 103). Chisel down to the line, then smooth the edge with a block plane and bevel slightly to meet the centreline. Fit this end in place, make a benchmark about a foot down the strip, bend the plank along the rest of the span and make another benchmark about a foot from where the uncut end will meet the centreline. Using this second benchmark as a reference, mark both edges of the uncut end about half an inch past the centreline. Connect the points with a straight edge, and chisel down to the line. When the plank is fitted back on the mould, this extra half inch slips under the lip of the previous plank, with a bit of extra clearance to allow for adjustment. When you are sure you have a good snug fit at both ends, remove the plank, add glue, and staple it in place. Continue with all the planks until the second side of the hull bottom is finished.

Some things can be understood only in the doing, and fitting the last plank falls into this category. You will probably have to rely on trial and error to shape the long angle so that it sits snugly in its niche. My approach is to lay a plank beside the opening, draw a benchmark for reference and use dividers at 1-inch intervals along the gap to measure the varying width. I transfer the divider points to the last strip (every 2 inches), join the points and cut along the line. Because the last plank cannot

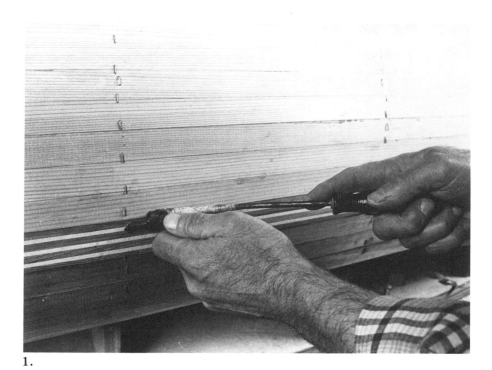

1.

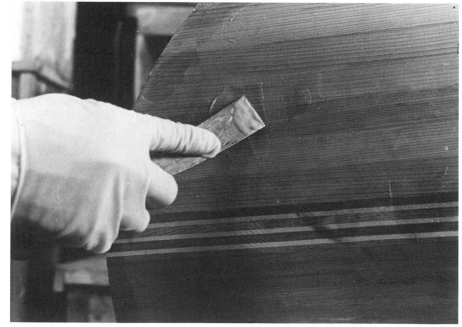

2.

3.

5.

4.

1. With the hull fully planked and the glue cured, carefully remove the staples. **2.** Fill the gaps between planks with a paste of epoxy glue and sanding dust. Then, when the filler has set, smooth the hull, **3,** into fluid curves with a block plane and spokeshave. **4.** A long plane should be used to smooth flat areas, especially along the centreline if you plan to install a keel. **5.** When the hull is roughly faired, sand it perfectly smooth with an orbital sander and #80 paper. Then, after wetting the hull to raise the grain and show up rough spots, finish sand with #120 paper.

be slipped under the cove edge of the second-last plank, that outside cove edge will have to be removed, leaving the inside lip to hold the last plank in place.

After the hull bottom is planked, the glue has to cure for about 12 hours. You are now about halfway through the whole project – a perfect time to sit back in your moaning chair, congratulate yourself and dream about someday paddling this craft down a mist-shrouded lake.

FAIRING THE HULL EXTERIOR

Tools:

staple puller
putty knife
block plane
spokeshave
jack plane
orbital sander
sanding block
vacuum cleaner

Materials:

epoxy glue
solvent
sanding dust
sandpaper #80, #120

Safety:

ventilation
gloves
mask

At this point, the hull may look somewhat rough, but it is undeniably canoelike despite the gaps between planks and rows of staples. The desire to rush ahead with the finishing process is natural now that your hull is beginning to take shape, but it is important to temper enthusiasm for progress with the reality that a smooth hull will only come after much sanding and planing. If you prepare yourself for the pace of finishing and accept that it can be as relaxing as it is monotonous, you will be able to enjoy the leisurely pace of the operation and to ensure that the canoe's finish will reach its full potential.

Before you begin to smooth the hull, of course, the staples must be pulled, and it is important not to bruise the wood while prying them loose. I use an old screwdriver bent at the end to provide leverage and taped at the bend to prevent scarring the wood.

Some people are compelled to fill the staple holes, and one homebuilder once tried gluing in hundreds of toothpicks to hide the holes, but nothing you do can make them disappear completely, so it is best to learn to love them, leaving them unfilled. They will be most visible in light woods, but if the staples were lined up, the effect can be pleasing. There is also a practical advantage in leaving them unfilled, as the glass cloth wicks resin into holes, adding to the bond between wood and epoxy.

Holes in the stems, however, and gaps in the planking must be filled. Mix epoxy filler (glue thickened to a paste with the cedar dust left over from ripping the planking

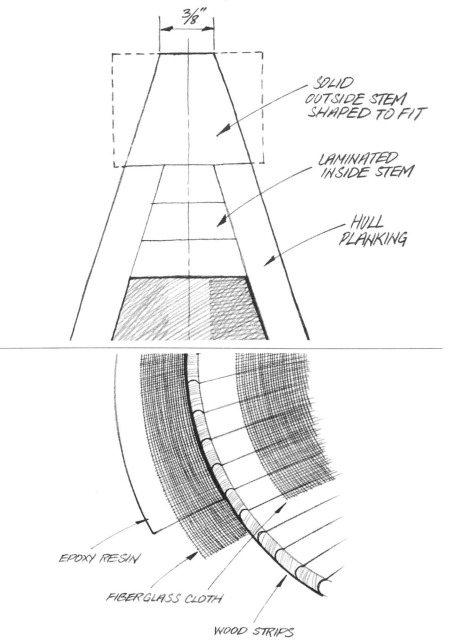

Top: *An outside stem is added to the planked hull's leading edge before the sheathing process is started.* **Bottom:** *The monocoque hull is wood sandwiched by layers of epoxy resin and fibreglass cloth.*

on the table saw), and proceed methodically over the entire surface of the hull, checking for imperfections or gaps in the planking, especially along the keel-line and bilge curve. With a putty knife, force the filler into the cracks, squeezing out air. Scrape off any excess, for what you smear on now will have to be sanded off later. Let the filler dry overnight.

If you want outside stems, fit them now, before the hull is faired, so they can be smoothed into the final sweeping curves of the canoe. Beginning at the bow, seat the untapered outside stem over the top of the inside stem. It should be slightly wider than the end it is covering. The outside stem will sit neatly near the sheer-line, but as it curves toward the keel-line, some of the cedar planking will have to be chiselled away to make a flat seat for it. (Be sure that the outside stem ends before the inside one, so that it will have a firm seating on the hull's bottom.) Screw the outside stem temporarily in place; then, to plan its final taper, run a pencil along the edges where it meets the planking on each side. Finally, draw a centreline down the stem's outside width. Remove the stem from the canoe and shape it with a plane or spokeshave from the marked outside edges toward the centreline, so that you achieve a ⅜-inch leading edge. If there is no keel, taper that end of the stem slightly so it blends smoothly with the hull. An attached keel, on the other hand, can be scarfed to merge with the outside stem.

After it is roughly shaped, screw the stem back on the canoe to make any final adjustments, then remove it, apply epoxy glue to the inside surfaces, and screw it permanently in place. These screws can be a nuisance when it comes time to install the brass stem-band — invariably, the stem-band holes seem to line up over at least one of the outside stem-screws. You can avoid this frustration by removing the stem screws after the glue is set and then filling the holes with cedar plugs, carved to fit and dipped in epoxy to seat them firmly.

Attach the outside stem to the stern in the same manner.

You are now ready to fair the hull, to smooth all those flat planks into fluid curves. With a block plane or spokeshave, remove any sharp edges that might lift the fibreglass cloth off the surface, trapping air. This is one time you cannot get away with anything less than a razor-sharp tool. Stop and resharpen whenever the blade starts to tear instead of cut. Work *with* the grain, being careful not to pick it up with your tool.

If you are installing a keel, use your longest plane to flatten the bottom of the hull at the centreline where the keel will sit.

When the rough edges are removed, sand the hull with an orbital sander or hand sanding block, using medium-grit #80 sandpaper. Hand sanding, though possible, requires the stamina of a purist.

Comments one who did it: "Never again. Some days, I just couldn't face it. It takes a long time and is not particularly fun. Power sanders do the job just as well without the drudgery." A disc sander with a 1½-inch-thick, 8-inch-diameter soft foam pad works extremely well, while an electric drill with sanding disc attachment is an acceptable alternative. A belt sander is also usable if you are careful that its edges do not dig in and that it does not cut too fast. Sand in the direction of the grain or at a slight angle to it. As you work, keep running your hand over the surface until all bumps and edges are reduced to soft curves. This outside sanding should take about three hours. A time-saving trick is to load four or five strips of sandpaper onto the sander at once. As the top one wears down, just rip it off and keep sanding, without having to stop and reload.

For a final finish with the best clarity, wipe the surface of the wood with a damp cloth so it is thoroughly wetted but not dripping. The water raises the compressed wood fibres and affords a sneak preview of the hull's appearance after the resin is applied. Poorly sanded, fibrous sections will absorb more water and show up as dark blotches. Where glue coats the wood, the water will not be absorbed, causing whitish spots. Check over the wet hull, and mark the areas that need more work. When the hull looks dry again, sand with #120. The more

finely the wood is sanded, the more consistent the finish colour will be. Dust off the hull with a vacuum cleaner, and let it rest overnight before beginning lay-up.

SHEATHING THE HULL (OUTSIDE)

Tools:

 3-inch natural-bristle
  paintbrush
 stir sticks
 mixing cans
 squeegee
 scissors
 utility knife

Materials:

 epoxy resin hardener
 solvent
 fibreglass cloth
 hand cleaner
 dry sandpaper #80
 wet sandpaper #240

Safety:

 gloves
 ventilation
 barrier cream

You have now reached a critical stage of construction. I admit to feeling a bit apprehensive each time before beginning lay-up, because it allows no breaks in the moaning chair — once you start, there is no turning back, starting over or even slowing down. It is probably one of the most difficult steps, but it is also one of the most exhilarating, as you watch the colours of the wood brighten and sparkle under the wet fibreglass.

The easy part is laying on the cloth. First, wipe down the hull with epoxy solvent to provide a clean, dust-free base. If your design does not include a keel, cut a 3-inch strip of cloth, and lay it over the keel-line so it extends partway down the curve of the stems. Being careful not to dislocate this narrow reinforcing strip, drape the large sheet of fibreglass over the canoe. It is easier if you can enlist a friend to hold the opposite corners of the fabric sheet — together, stretch it over the hull, and lower it into position. Since it is 60 inches wide and a foot longer than the canoe, the cloth should hang evenly below the sheer-line on both sides and extend a few inches past the stems. Working from amidships toward each stem, run your hands systematically over the canoe to stretch the fibreglass gently over the contours of the hull, smoothing wrinkles toward the stems. The cloth is fairly heavy yet has some give, so when it is wetted out, it should easily take the shape of the boat, with excess cloth gathered at the bow and stern, where it is later cut off.

The next step is wetting out the cloth with epoxy resin. Because of the fast-setting, indelible nature of epoxy, it is important to be well prepared before beginning. For this reason, we explain the process and the tricky techniques in detail before giving the actual instructions for the hull. You may want to practise with a scrap of cloth and a spare piece of wood before

sheathing the canoe itself.

Reread the section on temperature and humidity in the workplace (page 56). The temperature of the ingredients is just as important as the room and hull temperatures, so warm the resin and hardener to 90 to 100 degrees F, which makes them completely homogeneous when mixed together. A few minutes on a baseboard heater, in a hot-water bath or under heat lamps will make the epoxy thin and runny, so that it will soak quickly through the cloth into the surface fibres of the wood.

The resin and hardener are dispensed from mini-pumps — one shot of each delivers the materials in an accurate pre-measured ratio. Wearing hand protection, mix the two together in clean containers made of wax-free paper, plastic or metal. Do not use foam or glass containers, because the epoxy produces heat when the resin and hardener are mixed. Stir the epoxy for a full minute, not vigorously whipping in air, but steadily, scraping the sides of the container often.

The epoxy will stay fully liquid for about 15 minutes, then gradually begin to thicken. After 5 to 9 hours, it will be partially cured, no longer tacky to the touch, and after 15 to 20 hours, it can be sanded and shaped. The reaction may seem complete at this point, but a residual hardening will continue for about a week. The pot life of the resin (the length of time it remains liquid) can be extended by pouring the well-mixed epoxy into

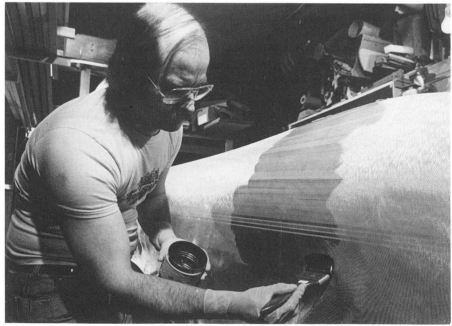

1.

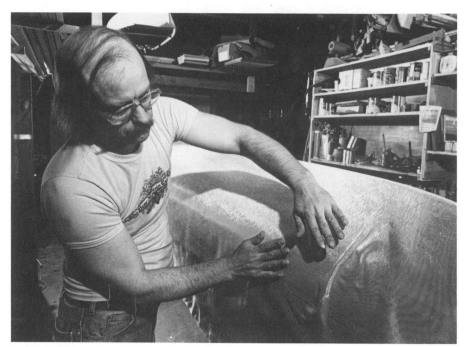

2.

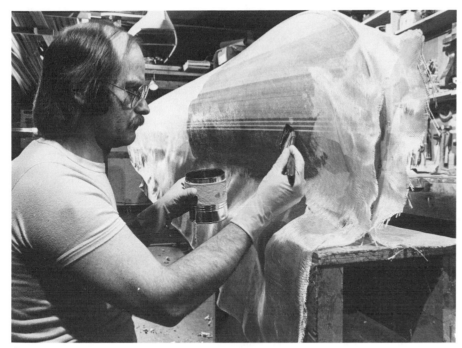

3.

4.

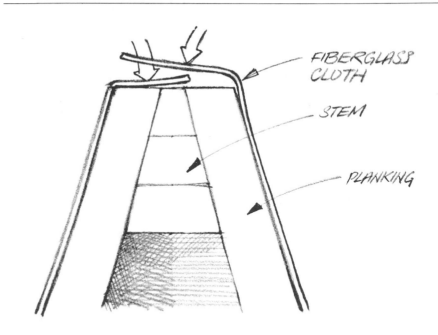

FIBERGLASS CLOTH

STEM

PLANKING

5.

1. *After draping the sheet of fibreglass over the hull, smooth out the wrinkles until the heavy cloth conforms neatly to the canoe's contours.* **2.** *Start wetting out the cloth with epoxy resin 2 to 3 feet aft of the bow. By working toward the stem first,* **3,** *any extra cloth will be smoothed toward the end fold, where it can be cut off.* **4.** *With the cloth secured at the bow quarter, wetting can proceed from keel to sheer, back toward the stern.* **5.** *At the stems, the cloth is cut and overlapped for a neat, wrinkle-free finish.*

(Note: This illustration has only an inside stem.)

1.

3.

2.

4.

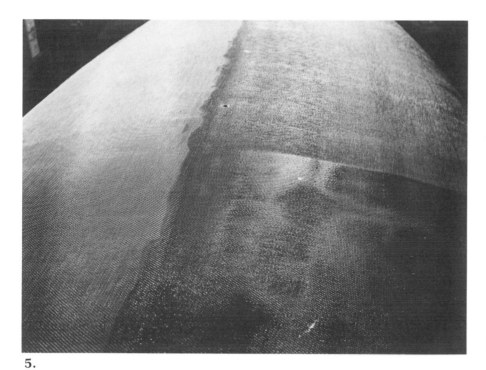

5.

1. *Keep the squeegee at a 75-degree angle, and use light but firm pressure to scrape across the top of the cloth without squeezing epoxy out of the fibre.* **2.** *Clean the excess resin off the squeegee by running it through a notch cut in a cardboard juice can.* **3. & 4.** *The effect of proper squeegeeing is obvious — while unscraped sections have bumps of resin and bubbles, the scraped sections are a smooth even texture.* **5 & 6.** *With one side wetted out, move to the opposite side. If the first section of epoxy begins to dry too quickly, go back and squeegee it before finishing the rest of the side.*

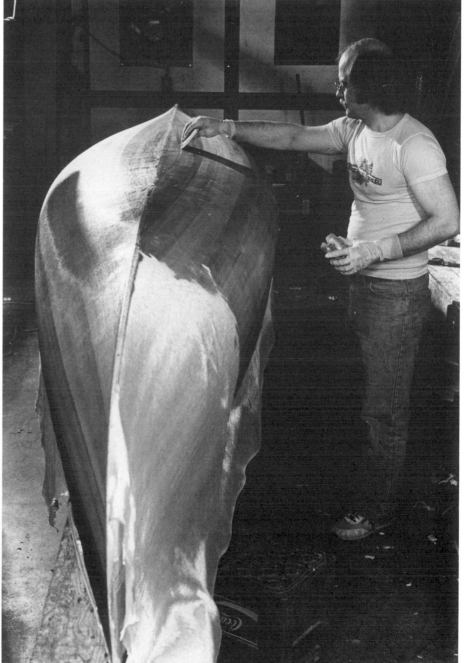

6.

a flat pie plate or paint roller pan. This helps to dissipate the chemical's catalytic heat produced by the reaction, making the epoxy thicken more slowly.

Applying the epoxy is not as easy as painting, but it is not difficult, providing that you understand the process and keep it under control at every stage. A squeegee is absolutely essential. It has a firm but flexible rubber edge that is perfect for applying resin. Nothing else works as well to smooth the epoxy over the hull and, later, to scrape away the excess.

To apply epoxy over a horizontal surface, pour a small puddle onto the cloth, then spread it gently with the squeegee. Use a stroking, not a back-and-forth painting, motion to move the epoxy gently over the surface. Do not work one area until the cloth is completely saturated. Leave it slightly flooded and move on, giving the resin time to soak in. A squeegee will not work on a vertical surface (inside the bow and sides), so saturate a brush with epoxy and stroke downwards. Spread the resin evenly and liberally, then move on to the next area, allowing it to soak in naturally. Trying to force the resin into the cloth will only beat in air.

Always work out from the wetted areas to keep the cloth from bunching up and wrinkling. If the resin dries quickly, it is critically important to maintain a wet edge so that ridges of thicker resin do not build up. If you have an assistant to mix small batches of resin

while you wet out the cloth, you will be able to keep that wet edge and will always have fresh resin for optimum saturation.

After the first coat of resin has had time to soak in (about 20 to 30 minutes or when it just begins to thicken), you will have to go over the entire hull with a squeegee, scraping off any excess and filling in starved areas. This technique is one of the trickiest parts of the process. The purpose is to produce an even coating of resin over the whole hull, pressing the cloth against the wood and removing excess resin and trapped air. Hold the tool towards you at an angle of about 75 degrees, and use light but firm pressure to scrape across the *top* of the cloth, discarding the excess as illustrated. It is better to take off too little than too much. When you push too hard, you starve the cloth, air is trapped in the weave by the next coat, and it remains visible.

Timing is critical here. The resin has to soak the cloth and surface wood fibres thoroughly, but it must not start to set up. If you squeegee too soon, the cloth may become starved because the wood is still absorbing resin. But if you squeegee too late, you will scrape up thick resin and the finish will whiten. Only experience can teach the proper timing, but as a rule of thumb, leave the resin a few more minutes if it still seems runny.

All together, three coats of epoxy will be applied to the outside of the hull. While the first bonds the

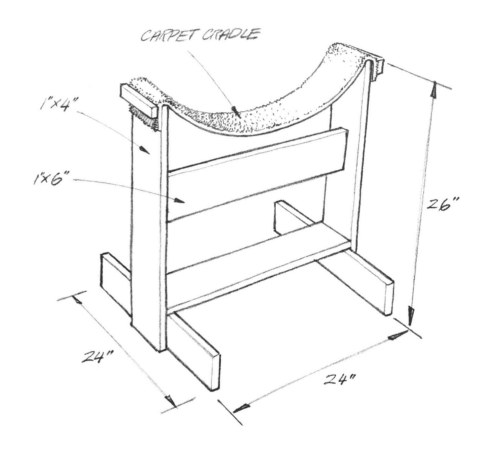

CARPET CRADLE

1"x4"

1"x6"

26"

24"

24"

Above: *Build a cradle to hold the hull once it has been taken from the mould.* **Right:** *It is easier to sand the hull when the canoe is resting on the cradle.* **Far right:** *After dry-sanding, smooth the epoxy to a silken finish by wet-sanding.*

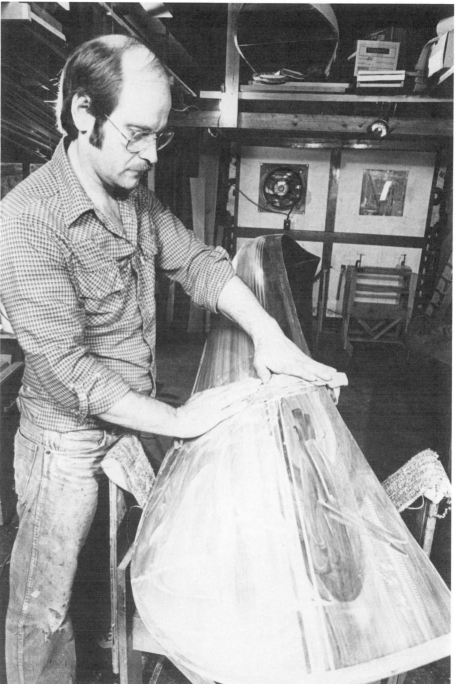

cloth to the wood, the second fills up the weave. At this stage, apply the epoxy with a squeegee, because a roller or brush will make the resin foam on the rough surface of the first coat. Pour a puddle on the surface, then force it into the weave with the squeegee, in the same manner as above.

The third coat buries the weave of the cloth and protects it, adding strength and durability to your canoe. It can be applied with a brush or roller, as the hull surface is now fairly smooth. (If you use a roller, apply a fourth coat, because the resin rolls on more thinly.) Be especially sure the resin is warm and runny, but take care to avoid runs because this is your finish coat. The more care you take with each application, the less sanding you will have in the end.

If possible, set aside a large chunk of time, and apply all three coats in one go. If you wait longer than three to four hours between coats, a residue will rise to the surface which has to be scrubbed off with water and Ajax (or any cleaner containing ammonia). After rinsing with water, quickly sand the hull with #80 paper (being careful not to expose or weaken the fabric), then wipe down with acetone before the next coat can be applied. Applying each coat when the one underneath is tacky may take you from one dawn to the next, but it produces a better sheath and is less work in the long run.

The time has come to begin lay-up in earnest. Be as neat and clean as possible. Apply barrier cream to your hands, and wear disposable rubber gloves. Keep rags handy for wiping up spills before they harden, and be sure to clean your hands and tools after each coat is applied.

Mix up the first batch of epoxy, using four shots each of resin and hardener. The cloth will soak it up rapidly, so you will use up these large batches quickly. Stir the mixture thoroughly, then pour it into a pie plate or paint roller pan (a rag wrapped around the mixing container will catch the drips). Start 2 to 3 feet aft of the bow, and apply the resin in that quarter first (page 110), working from the centre of the hull out toward the bow, keel-line to gunwale. Do not worry about the cloth sliding around — its own weight should keep it fairly snug on the hull — providing that you flow the epoxy on gently, as described. Wet out to the stem edge, smoothing the cloth down gently to bring it over as much of the curve as possible. There will be a fold of cloth that stands out from the stem, but don't worry about that now. Return to the point at which you started (it should be wet), and start working toward the stern, moving from the keel to the gunwale on one side of the canoe only.

To ensure a flawless finish, it is important to squeegee the resin before it dries, as a ridge of epoxy will build up and leave a noticeable mark on the hull if it dries too soon. By squeegeeing from the keel to gunwale and watching out for side flows of resin onto drier areas, ridges will be avoided. As you wet out one side of the canoe, check to see if the first applications are ready to squeegee. You should be able to wet out the whole side before returning to the beginning to scrape off the excess resin as described. When the first side is done, continue in the same sequence to wet out the other side.

When both sides are wetted and squeegeed, carefully trim the fibreglass at the bow so it extends past the stem — ⅜ inch on one side and ¾ to 1 inch on the other (page 111). Brush some fresh resin down the stem, then carefully fold the short side over with your brush, pressing it tightly in place. Then wrap the other side around, being careful not to push the first lap out of position. Gently squeegee off any excess resin without disturbing the lap. After finishing the stern stem in the same manner, check the hull for runs, bubbles and lifts. And as the first coat cures, keep an eye on the stem overlaps. They may tend to lift at first, but as the resin gets tacky, they will stay in place.

While you wait for the first coat to set up, wipe up spills and clean off your tools. Scrape excess resin off your brush, rinse well in solvent, then soak in fresh solvent until it is needed again. When the epoxy is firm, trim the excess cloth close to the sheer-line with a sharp utility knife. (If your canoe design calls for a keel, fasten it at this point. Turn to page 132 for instructions.)

After three to four hours, the first coat of epoxy will be sufficiently cured to stabilize the cloth but tacky enough to provide a good bond for the second coat. Mix smaller batches of resin and hardener (two shots each). Because this coat just fills in the weave, each batch will stretch farther. Apply the second coat with a squeegee as described, systematically covering the hull in the same sequence as above.

When the second coat is tacky, apply the third coat with a brush. Batches can be three shots each, since the brush lays on the epoxy more thickly. If you prefer, use a roller to apply a third and a fourth finish coat. Whichever method you use, watch for runs in the epoxy (this is where good lighting is essential), and try to keep the thickness of the finish coat consistent.

For a quicker, complete cure that assures a perfectly clear lay-up, it helps greatly to warm up the hull 24 hours after the final coat is applied. With a hot-air gun, heat the surface gently until it is quite warm to the touch (120 to 140 degrees F). Hold the gun about a foot from the hull, moving it constantly to avoid overheating any one spot. A hair dryer makes a good substitute but takes much longer.

Be prepared for a letdown when the outside lay-up is complete. The hull you took such pains to fit and smooth and sand is now buried

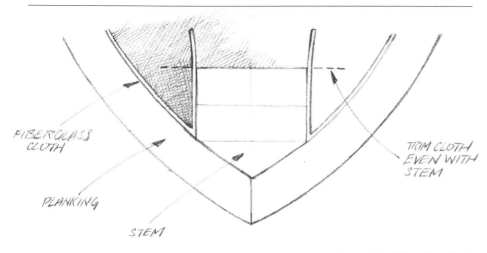

FIBERGLASS CLOTH

PLANKING

STEM

TRIM CLOTH EVEN WITH STEM

Above: *Fitting the cloth around the inside stem is an exacting task. When the whole inside surface of the hull is wetted out and squeegeed, slit the cloth over the inside stem, and work it into the cracks on either side, as shown. After the epoxy is firm, the cloth is trimmed flush with the top of the stem.* **Right:** *Add a thick pad of foam under the paper on the sander for fairing the inside of the hull to allow the sandpaper,* **below,** *to follow the curve of the hull.*

under a layer of lumpy plastic. Do not despair — sanding will smooth out those runs and bumps, clarifying any milkiness produced by the excess density of the resin layer. There is still some work ahead, but take consolation in the thought that the wood is now protected and your canoe has gained immeasurably in strength and durability.

When the hull is cured, dry-sand with #80 grit, then wet down the hull, and use wet sanding paper to get a perfectly smooth finish. If you have been diligent in applying a smooth sheath of epoxy, free of runs and sags, this will not be a difficult job, but it will be a dirty one. A dust mask and good ventilation are imperative. You may find that

the areas near the sheer are easier to sand once the hull is off the mould.

Removing the Hull From the Mould

Raising your boat to its rightful upright position is one of the highlights of the canoe-building process. That first glimpse will repay all your hard work and keep you going until the finished canoe slides into the water.

While the final resin coat is curing, prepare a cradle to hold the canoe steady for the inside lay-up and trim installation. Several large cardboard cartons cut to fit the hull bottom will make a quick temporary support. For a sturdier base, shape two pieces of wood to the hull curve, cover with foam or carpet, and tack them to sawhorses. If you plan to build more than one canoe, or want to store the boat this way, build a permanent cradle (page 114). Whatever form it takes, the support should raise the canoe so the gunwales are just above your belt line.

When the hull is cured and sanded, enlist a friend to help lift it off the strongback. Begin by removing the screws fixing the bow and stern moulds to the stems. If your canoe has a curved bow profile, you will have to reach inside, unscrew the bow and stern mould sections from their station blocks and slide them back along the strongback out of the way. The hull should lift off easily if the moulds were well waxed. With one person at each stem, lift firmly and evenly to loosen the hull. Watch carefully as you lift; if the hull sticks, try to determine where, and tap the adhering mould from inside. If the hull will not come off, unscrew the offending moulds from their station blocks, and lift it off with the moulds inside. You should not have trouble dislodging them once the canoe is upright.

FAIRING THE INSIDE OF THE HULL

Tools:

spokeshave
block plane
sanding block
disc sander
putty knife
tack cloth

vacuum cleaner

Materials:

epoxy filler
sandpaper #80 and #120

Safety:

dust mask
safety goggles
ventilation

Your boat is finally in its seagoing stance, but there is still much to do before it can be christened. Take a look inside the hull. If you were diligent in wiping off the glue as you planked, sanding this surface will not be formidable. Still, most amateur builders find this stage the least pleasant because it is dusty, uncomfortable and frustrating to work on the awkward inside curves. But as you will have learned by now, the clarity of the glassed surface is well worth the effort required to smooth the wood properly.

If the keel was fastened with temporary screws, remove them now. Fill these holes (and any other flaws) with filler made from epoxy glue and sanding dust. Be as neat as possible — the filler will not sand as easily as the wood.

Smooth the inside of the hull just as you did the outside, shaving off the sharp ridges with a spokeshave, then sanding with #80 paper. Visually, you can get away with more flaws on the inside, but you cannot overlook the stepped edges between planks. A disc sander (a drill with a 4-inch foam sanding pad) will reduce hand-

sanding on the curves that cannot accommodate the shaving tools or orbital sander. (The orbital sander will take inside curves better if you add a thick pad of foam just under the sandpaper.) Use enough pressure to bend the backing pad into the shape being sanded. Keep the machine moving to avoid sanding flat spots into the curves. Caution is needed here: unless you are used to handling a disc sander, it can chew up your boat in a hurry. To avoid the dust of sanding, the inside surface can also be planed smooth with a convex-soled plane. Finish by wetting down the inside, letting it dry and hand-sanding with #120 sandpaper. Vacuum out the inside surface, and wipe down with a tack cloth to pick up any remaining dust particles.

SHEATHING THE INSIDE

Tools:

3-inch paintbrush
mini-pump dispenser
squeegee   scissors
mixing cans   utility knife
stir sticks   rags

Materials:

fibreglass cloth
resin and hardener
solvent
wet sandpaper #240
dry sandpaper #80

Safety:

gloves   ventilation
mask   barrier cream

Your experience in fibreglassing

the outside of the hull should help make this step easier, although the inside curves require special attention.

Carefully lower a full layer of cloth into the hull. Smooth out all the wrinkles, working out from the centre to each stem. Trim it roughly to length, letting the sides overhang. The basic principles of mixing and applying the resin are the same inside as out. Remember especially that the resin should be warm, well-mixed but not overworked and that you must keep a wet edge at all times.

The bulk of the lay-up inside can be done with a squeegee. Mix a four-shot batch of resin and hardener. Pour a puddle into the canoe bottom in the bow quarter, and drag it up the side with a squeegee, wetting out the inside of the hull in the same sequence as you did the outside. Do not worry about a finished appearance at this stage, just float on the resin. In the bow and stern stem sections, apply the epoxy with a brush, and pay particular attention when you squeegee off the excess later. When both sides are wetted and squeegeed, cut a slit in the cloth over the full length of both inside stems. With the squeegee, work the cloth smoothly down into the crack between the stem and the hull and then up the side of the stem (page 117).

Wait until the first coat is firm, then use a utility knife to trim the cloth even with the stems, sanding lightly to smooth its edges. Then cut off the excess cloth around the sheer. Squeegee on the second coat, brushing resin over the stems and the cut edge of the cloth. Let it cure three to four hours until tacky. If weight is a consideration, two coats are adequate on the inside. It leaves a slightly toothed surface that is not as slippery as a fine finish, but you will still be able to see the weave of the cloth. For a glossier, tougher (though heavier and more slippery) inside finish, brush on a third coat or roll on two more coats or resin.

When the hull is fully cured, sand the inside to smooth the surface and prepare it for varnishing. If you applied only two coats of resin, scrub the hull with ammonia cleaner, rinse well, and sand only the rough imperfections (too much sanding could expose the cloth fibres). With three or more coats on the inside, dry-sand the surface with #80 sandpaper, then wet-sand with #240 for a fine finish. Wipe down the hull, both inside and out, with acetone or lacquer thinner.

Except for a protective coat of varnish, the hull is finished. Rushton used to sell canoes like this as "shells," so that paddlers could trim the boats to their own satisfaction. That pleasure will be all yours — but if you plan to fit out this shell in a leisurely way, remember to keep it out of direct sunlight. After all the effort you have put into producing a bright finish, it would be a disaster of no small magnitude for the sun to cloud it.

TROUBLE-SHOOTING

The following chart details some of the most common problems encountered in the woodstrip/resin construction method, their symptoms and causes. Read the chart *before* beginning to build: Prevention is a lot easier than fixing a botched job.

Symptom	Cause	Prevention/Cure
Strongback twists out of square.	Wet wood drying.	Place weights on the feet, preferably before it happens.
One entire mould too small (obvious during fairing).	Improper tracing or cutting out of mould.	Slide mould toward closest end until it fairs in smoothly.
Woodstrips crack or break during ripping.	Poor-quality wood with checks, shakes, cross grain.	Dispose of defective strips; splice strips during planking process.
Planking springs out of alignment on mould.	Square edge planks with butt joints. Too much compound bend.	Staple between stations. Drive ½-inch #4 screw and washer into mould. Install tapered cheater plank to relieve tension at stem.
Planks break in compound bends.	Cross grain. Too much tension.	Find strip with straighter grain. Use cheater plank.
Gaps between planking.	Improper fit; planks breaking or chipping along edges.	Fill with epoxy glue/sanding dust filler.
Planks "shingle."	Planks not landing fair to mould; inaccurate stem bevel.	Stop planking until problem solved; install brads, screw/washers, cheater strips.
Resin turns cloudy or thick during mixing.	Resin too cold. Outdated material.	Prewarm resin. If cloudy even when mixed warm, check shelf life and contact distributor.
Runs in epoxy between coats.	Too much resin.	Squeegee if still green; scrape off with cabinet scraper if still tacky; sand or scrape off if cured.

Symptom	Cause	Prevention/Cure
Cloth shifts during lay-up.	Excessive working of resin.	Work resin gently with patting squeegee motion; do not brush.
Cloth lifts off hull as resin curing.	Excess resin "floating" cloth.	Squeegee.
	Excess cloth hanging in such a way that cloth pulls away at edges.	Trim cloth.
Cloth lifts off stem overlap.	Resin not sticky enough.	Push down periodically with squeegee until resin tacky.
	Cloth under tension.	Cut gussets around curve.
Uneven resin coat.	Improper squeegeeing.	Sand to even thickness, but do not damage cloth; if fewer than three coats remain after sanding, apply another coat.
Weave of cloth visible after final coat.	Incomplete wetting out of cloth due to cold or partially set-up resin.	Heat ingredients before mixing; use fresh, small batches.
	Cloth starved by squeegeeing too hard or insufficient resin.	Less pressure on squeegee; more resin on first coat.
Epoxy cloudy as it cures.	Air introduced by overworking resin.	Use proper squeegee technique.
	Air trapped in resin-starved cloth.	Use proper wetting-out or squeegee technique.
	Resin too thick (low temperature).	Heat ingredients; maintain proper humidity.
	Resin too thick (started to set up).	Use fresh batches; squeegee before set-up.
	Moisture contamination.	Live with it; paint it. If cloudy only in one spot, let cure, then treat as repair.
White spots in glassed surface.	Glue/filler smears prevent absorption of resin into wood fibres.	Prevent by proper sanding; live with it or treat as repair.
Finish clouds after curing.	Ultraviolet deterioration.	Prevent by covering hull between lay-up and varnishing.
	Improper cure (workshop temperature too low).	Work in warm shop; warm hull with heat gun if temperature borderline; once cloudy, live with it, paint it or repair.
	Lay-up too thick.	Clarity may improve with sanding.
Fibreglassed hull looks blotchy, dark and light patches in wood.	Incomplete sanding of planking.	Prevent by wetting down and fine sanding before lay-up; no cure

CHARACTER DEVELOPMENT

Installing the Trim

"It has long been an axiom of mine that the little things are infinitely the most important."

— Sherlock Holmes
Copper Beeches

An untrimmed hull, while not an unattractive shape, is, as one waggish canoeist observed, like a matron without a corset — badly in need of rigidity and structure in a few key places.

It is an apt comparison, as your finished hull is stable at the stems and below the waterline, but its untrimmed flanks near the sheer-edge still need some additional support. What it needs most are gunwales to stiffen it from stem to stem, and thwarts, seats and decks to add crosswise strength.

The sequence for attaching most of the trim is not carved in stone, but the inwales are always installed first to provide that basic bow-to-stern support. The centre thwart is

fixed temporarily to establish the proper midship width, then the decks are fastened, followed by the outwales. The seats and thwarts should be fitted temporarily (either before or after the outwales), as they have to be removed while the inside of the hull is varnished.

As you read through the directions for installing the trim, there may seem to be a formidable amount of measuring, clamping and double-checking. But experienced boatbuilders will agree that there is no such thing as being too careful. Working well into the wee hours with a portable television or a blasting stereo for distraction can lead to painful mistakes if your concentration is broken long

enough to glue an inwale on backwards. Normally, an epoxy joint is forever, so mistakes are corrected only by several hours of chiselling and sanding the glue and wood left after the inwale or deck has been destroyed during removal. Such mistakes are seldom repeated, but it is better to avoid them completely.

INWALES

Tools:

hacksaw/coping saw
clamps
glue brush
drill
screwdriver
block plane
pencil

Materials:

epoxy glue
solvent
½-inch #4 noncorrosive flat head screws

Safety:

gloves

The inwales follow the sheerline of the canoe from bow to stern, so the more the design swoops up at the stems, the more difficult it will be to bend the inwales to shape. Starting at midships, clamp the first inwale very slightly below the edge of the hull, then continue toward each stem. The smooth, shallow arc of the top of the inwale will become the up-

1.

1. *Having clamped the inwale at midships and fit it temporarily to the sheer curve so that both ends of the wood extend past the stems, mark the correct angle of cut so that the inwale will mate neatly with the inside stem.* **2.** *If the bow rises sharply, you may have to force the inwale into position by clamping its end to a board laid across the stem. Then clamp the rest of the inwale along the sheer slightly below the top edge of the hull.* **3.** *Once fitted, unclamp three-quarters of the inwale's length, apply glue to the hull face, and clamp the inwale back into position. Then glue the final quarter length.* **4.** *When the inwale is glued and clamped, drill a pilot hole through the hull and partway into the inwale — then fasten with a flat head screw.* **5.** *When the glue has set, remove the clamps and plane the top edge of the hull flush with the inwale.*

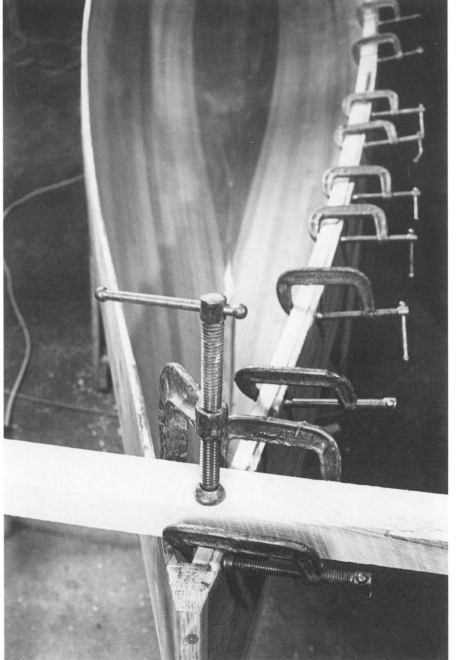

2.

3.

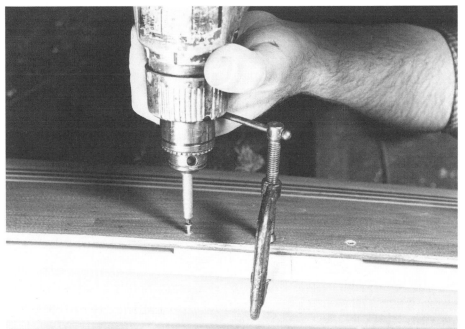

4.

5.

per limit of the boat, with the irregularities of the fibreglassed planking sanded down to meet it. Cut one end to size with a fine-tooth hacksaw or coping saw, clamp it in place, and trim the other to fit, remembering to angle the ends so they fit snugly against the stem. If the inwale resists a hard, fast bend at the stem, draw the end up by clamping it to a board laid across the stem (page 124). When the inwale is fitted, sand the irregular hull edge flush.

Remove the clamps from three-quarters of the clamped inwale, and let it drape over the side of the hull. Spread the hull-side face of the inwale with epoxy glue, and clamp it back into place. Next remove the clamps from the unglued quarter, apply glue, and clamp back in place. Predrill from the hull into the inwale every 6 to 10 inches, and fasten with ½-inch #4 noncorrosive flat head screws, drawn in flush with the hull. Wipe off any excess glue, and repeat with the other inwale.

When the glue is set, plane the hull flush with the top of the inwale. Mark the screw positions on the top of the inwale with a light pencil so you will not hit them with the outwale screws.

CENTRE THWART

Tools:

back saw
clamps

Cut the centre thwart of length according to the specified width of the hull. If the canoe has plumb sides, the cut will be square, but if the sides are tumblehome or flared, the angle on the ends of the thwart must fit the curve of the hull. Spread the sides, and fit the thwart, clamping it temporarily in position under the inwales. This will ensure the proper width for fitting the decks. The thwart is not attached permanently until everything else is secure so that it can be positioned at the proper balance point for portaging.

DECKS

Tools:

block plane
spokeshave
screwdriver
utility knife
glue brush
drill/countersink bit

Materials:

sandpaper #80
2-inch #8 noncorrosive
　flat head screws
1½-inch #8 noncorrosive
　flat head screws
epoxy glue
solvent

Safety:

gloves

Although you may have already machined your decks (page 75), they require accurate dry-fitting before being glued in place. Fit one deck between the inwales at the stem, checking for a snug fit along

1.

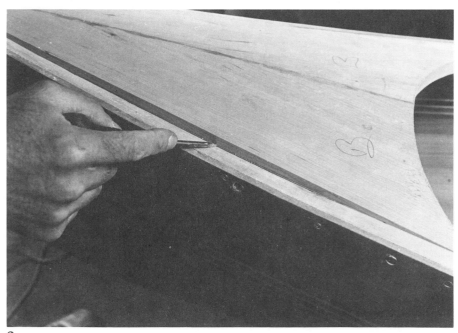

2.

3.

5.

4.

1. *Thwarts, like seats, are cut to size by laying them across the canoe to draw the correct cutting angle, and then bevelling the cut so the ends follow the curve of the hull.* **2.** *A flat deck fitted to a curved sheer will rise above the curve of the inwale. Prior to shaping the deck, clamp it in place, and trace along the inwale with an awl.* **3.** *Once marked, secure the deck in the clamping jig, and use a block plane to plane it down to the awl line.* **4.** *Finish it with a cabinet scraper, rather than sandpaper, if it is hardwood.* **5.** *Properly shaped, the lines of the deck become part of the overall symmetry of the canoe.*

Top left: *If your deck has a coaming, its edges must be shaped to fit the inwales before it is glued into place on the deck. While a feathered coaming simply needs to be smoothed into the inside of the inwales, the coaming shown here,* **bottom left**, *overlaps both the inwale and outwale. After cutting a rough notch in the coaming so that it seats over the gunwales, screw the coaming back to the deck and check the fit, marking any areas that need readjustment. After the coaming has been glued and screwed onto the deck, wooden plugs,* **above**, *can be used to cover the screw heads if the holes were counterbored.* **Facing page:** *Outwales are clamped to the hull starting at midships. They should extend past the stems and sit level with the inwales. Because the decks will not accommodate clamps, tie the outwales into the hull with screws at the bow and stern. (Note that the seats can be installed before attaching the outwales, although they must be removed before varnishing the inside of the hull.)*

its full length. Predrill through the hull and inwale into the widest part of the deck on either side. Fasten with 2-inch #8 screws. Keeping the deck firmly in position, continue toward the stem, fastening enough screws on each side to secure the deck without gaps (four per side should be enough). As the deck and inwales converge towards the stem, reduce the screw size to 1½-inch #8. Repeat for the other deck.

If the sheer-line rises toward the stems, a flat deck will have to be shaped to match this curve (page 75). Fit the deck at its widest part and at the stem, then scribe its sides with an awl guided along the curve of the inwale. Remove the deck, and secure it in the gluing jig. Using a spokeshave, block plane and cabinet scraper, shape it down to the scribed line, giving its top surface a pleasing crown or camber (page 127). After it is shaped, refit the deck. At the stem and front edges, the deck will touch the inwales for a full ¾-inch depth, but in between, the gluing surface will be reduced. This is not important as long as there is still enough of a mating surface between deck and inwale. Make any final adjustments, then sand the deck smooth.

When both decks have been accurately dry-fitted, unscrew them, and mix up a batch of epoxy glue using one shot each of resin and hardener. Brush epoxy on all mating surfaces of one deck, then screw it firmly in place. Repeat with the other deck. Remember to wipe off any excess glue, inside and out.

If your deck has a coaming, it will have been dry-fitted when the decks were machined but removed while the deck was being fitted between the outwales. Now that the decks are permanently installed in the canoe, a *feathered* coaming can be glued and screwed firmly back into place. If the coaming is to overlap, it should be trimmed and glued permanently after the outwales are installed.

With both decks in place, you can now round off the inside edges of the inwales with a plane and #80 sandpaper or router.

OUTWALES

Tools:

countersink bit or counterbore
  and plug
drill
clamps
screwdriver
glue brush
chisel
plane

Materials:

1½-inch #8 noncorrosive
  flat head screws
sandpaper #80, #120 and #220
epoxy glue
solvent

Safety:

gloves

There are two options for attaching the outwales: You can countersink flat head screws in flush with

the surface of the outwale, or counterbore and cover the screw heads with a wooden plug. The latter takes a little more time but is very nautical and seals the fastener inside the wood. In either case, start amidships by clamping one outwale to the outside of the hull, making sure it extends slightly past both stems. Make benchmarks, then remove. Mix a batch of epoxy glue, and apply it to the hull-side of the outwale. Then clamp it back in position, drill through it and the hull into the inwale at about 10-inch intervals, taking care not to drill where you marked the location of the inwale screws. Counterbore if you are using plugs. Fasten the outwale to the hull with screws long enough to extend half or three-quarters of the way into the inwale. Draw the screws tightly so the glue begins to squeeze out, but not so tightly that the outwale splits. Wipe off any excess, then trim the outwale flush with the stem, and round off to your taste. Fasten the other outwale in the same manner.

When gluing in plugs, be sure to line up the grain in the plug with the grain in the outwale. Tap them just enough to seat them, but don't break the fibres of the plug. When the glue is set, trim the plugs with a sharp chisel so they are flush with the outwale. Shave them a little at a time to avoid splitting below the surface.

The permanent trim has all been installed, since seats and thwarts must be removable for varnishing now and in the future. Round off the rough edges on decks and gunwales with a router or plane and #80 sandpaper, then raise the highlights of the wood with a fine finish. Sand it all thoroughly with #120 paper, wet the wood to raise the fibres, then finish sand with #220 paper.

SEATS

Tools:

   clamps
   seat jig
   square edge
   coping saw
   drill
   countersink
   counterbore and plugs

Materials:

   carriage bolts *or* machine screws
   spacer blocks

The seats will normally be hung from the inwales, rather than being fastened to the hull, in order to allow the canoe to flex evenly under stress, but there are decisions to be made before you install your seats.

When buying a manufactured canoe, one has to accept the off-the-rack average, but not only is this canoe aesthetically your creation, it should also be made to measure for your legs and arms. The seats should be high enough so you can paddle comfortably and can easily get your feet out from under them. But you must also take into consideration the fact that the

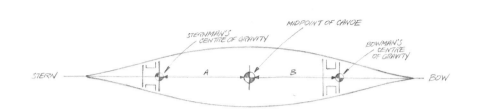

Sternman's weight x A equals Bowman's weight x B

Above: *Calculate seat positions with this formula if two paddlers of very different weights will be regularly using the canoe.* **Below:** *A seat jig will hold the seat frame in position for easier installation. Note the sliding measuring stick — two strips of wood clamped in the middle — for calculating the inside widths of the hull. When fitting the seat frames,* **facing page, top,** *determine the angle of the cut by laying the seat across the gunwales, taking the slope of the sides into account. With the jig in place,* **facing page, bottom,** *position the seat, and fasten it to the inwale using a dowel to maintain the correct space between the frame and the inwale.*

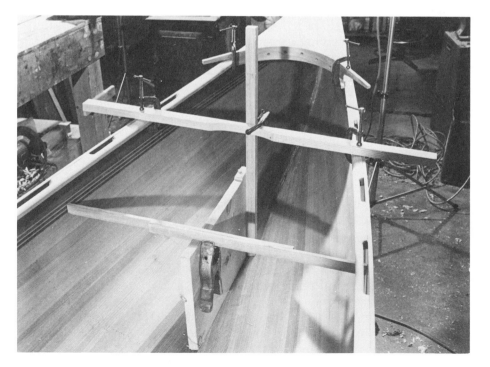

lower the centre of gravity, the more stable the canoe will be.

Obviously, the placement of seats depends on the paddler, his gear and the design of the canoe. Positioning seats close to the ends, where the width is narrow, allows easier paddling and maximum steering leverage. Placing the seats closer to the centre enables a canoe to ride over waves more easily and provides bow paddlers with more leg room. In any case, the end result should be a level canoe when paddlers and gear are aboard. Since paddlers are likely to change, most builders fasten the seats so they are equidistant from the centre and rely on the placement of gear to trim the canoe level. If you want to position the seats exactly for two specific paddlers, use the formula provided (page 130). Its use is most appropriate for two canoeists of vastly different weights. Note that both lines A and B are measured from the front of either seat.

There are two devices quickly made from scrap lumber that will greatly simplify seat installation. The seat jig is merely a plank that, when set on its edge, holds the seats steady at the correct height from the floor of the canoe while they are being fitted and attached. The sliding measuring stick is even more basic, consisting of two lengths of wood that can be extended or shortened to find the distance between the sides of the hull — when the correct length is established, they are simply clamped together.

Begin by positioning the jig for the stern seat. Measure along each inwale from the stem to the back of the seat. Clamp a 1 x 1-inch board across the inwales on the stem side of these points to ensure that the seat is positioned squarely between the gunwales. Now clamp the jig to the midpoint of this bar so that the bottom of the jig is resting along the keel-line of the canoe.

Because the canoe widens as it approaches amidships, the front members of the stern seat frame will have to be slightly longer than the back members. To determine the dimensions accurately, set the sliding measuring stick on the front edge of the seat jig, and expand it to touch the hull sides. Then centre it on the front edge of the seat frame, and mark the length. Repeat for the back members of the seat.

You now know where to cut off the frame, but not the cutting angle, either across its width or down its depth. It may be done by eye. Lay the seat frame across the gunwales, flush to the one-by-one and directly over the jig. Lay a straight edge over the cutting marks, and mark an angle parallel to that of the outwale. Also estimate the bevel required to match the slope of the hull side. Cut the seat frame to length at the proper angles, and set it on the jig. Cut four spacer blocks or dowels to fit between the seat frame and the inwales. If the canoe's sheer-line rises toward the stem, you will

have to determine the difference in height between the two spacers to ensure that the seat is level. Drill a hole slightly larger than the bolt through the centre of each spacer, then set the spacers in place, and drill a hole through the inwale to fit the bolt snugly. Let the bit move through the spacer hole to mark the top of the seat frame. Remove the spacers, and drill holes slightly larger than the bolts, through the frames, at these marks. Sand off any rough edges.

This process is repeated for the bow seat, except the jig's position will be reversed and the back members of the seat frame will be slightly longer than the front.

Assemble the seat frames and spacers, and fasten together with 3/16-inch carriage bolts or machine screws. If carriage bolts are used, the dome-shaped heads will extend above the inwale. If machine screws (flat head stove bolts) are used, they should be either countersunk flush or counterbored and plugged, with the bolt heads set in epoxy glue so they will not turn under the plugs when the seats are removed for occasional varnishings. After the seats are assembled, cut the bolts off at the nut, and file any sharp edges.

THWARTS

Structurally, a canoe up to 18 feet needs only one thwart, positioned in the centre. An extra thwart installed aft of the centre thwart is common in canoes over 16 feet, but its position is not as critical. All are bolted directly to the inwales, like the seats, but without spacers. With the centre thwart already clamped temporarily in position, install any remaining thwarts. Then, with one person on either side, pick the canoe up by the centre thwart to check its balance. Adjust the thwart back and forth until the stern is just slightly heavier than the bow, an important consideration to accommodate portaging. Drill through the inwale into the thwart, and bolt them together, two bolts on either side. Treat bolt heads the same as those for the seats.

KEEL

Tools:

| table saw | taut line |
| block plane | glue brush |

Materials:

epoxy glue
solvent
1/2-inch #4 screws
two finishing nails

Safety:

gloves

Ideally, the keel should be installed after the first coat of epoxy is brushed on the outside of the hull, so that subsequent coats cover and protect it. Because time is limited between epoxy coats, the keel should be dry-fitted just before lay-up begins. Begin by cutting the machined keel to length, long enough to be fastened into both

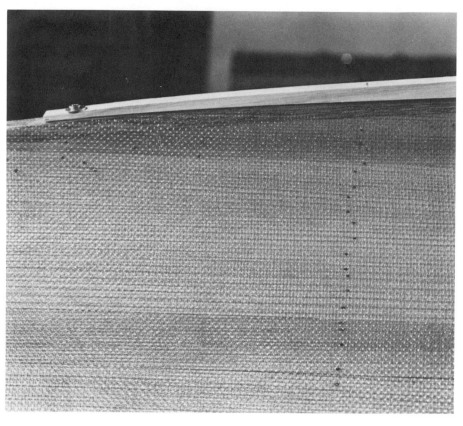

Above: *After the keel has been dry-fitted and its ends have been tapered to flow smoothly into the stems at bow and stern (if the canoe has outside stems), glue it into position, and fasten each end with a 1/2-inch screw, **facing page, top**. While the glue is drying, sight down the keel to check for straightness, **facing page, bottom**, tapping the keel into line until it is perfectly true.*

stems. Then cut a taper on either end so it will merge smoothly with the stems. If your hull has outside stems, taper the keel into its contoured end, so the stem and keel fit neatly together. Obviously, if there is only an inside stem, the keel can only taper down to the hull. Since the top of the keel has already been shaped to take a stem band 3/8 inch wide, the taper is cut from the wider 7/8-inch base (page 73). Measure back 16 inches from each end of the keel, and draw a taper from this point to the ends, rising from the wide, flat hull-side of the keel to within 1/8 inch of the shaped, narrow edge. Cut the wedge roughly on the table saw, then plane down to the taper line.

Position the keel over the centreline on the hull bottom, and make any necessary final adjustments in shaping. This process will be largely a matter of judgment and depends on the particular design of your canoe. The purpose is to create a smooth flow of line from the keel into each stem.

Installing the keel is a two-man job. Have your helper hold it firmly in position while you predrill and fasten a ½-inch #4 screw and washer through each end and into the stems. Remove the screws and keel, and proceed with the first coat of epoxy. The keel can be attached as soon as the epoxy is firm enough to work on. If everything goes smoothly and you keep moving, you can attach the keel before the first coat loses its tackiness. First, spread epoxy glue liberally on the underside of the keel, reposition it on the hull, and replace the stem screws. Then predrill and fasten a long finishing nail into the middle of the keel near each end, and stretch a taut line between the two nails. With your helper positioning the keel directly under the taut line, crouch under the canoe and predrill through the hull into the keel, using the planking seam as your guide. Be careful not to drill right through the keel. Starting in the centre and working out toward each stem, drive a ½-inch #4 screw between each station, while your helper holds the keel in position and checks for straightness. You can either use permanent brass screws or temporary screws that can be removed (and their holes filled) after the hull

comes off the moulds. Scrape off the excess glue, and wipe the keel down with a solvent. Sight down the length of the keel. If minor waves are apparent, set a block of wood beside the keel, and tap it gently into position.

Apply the second coat of epoxy, brushing it over the hull and keel, but leaving the keel-ends bare where they join the stem. By the time the second coat is firm, the glue on the keel will be set so the screws fastening the keel to the stem on the outside can be removed. Plug the hole with a little piece of wood, whittled to fit and dipped in epoxy, then cut it off flush. Dress the two keel-stem joints to a feather edge with a plane or spokeshave, being careful to keep the top edge crisp for the stem band. Apply the third coat of epoxy over the entire hull. Touch up the dressed ends of the keel with an extra coat of epoxy later, when laying up the inside.

If there isn't enough time to fasten the keel between the first and second coats, leave it until lay-up is complete and the hull sanded. It is more important to get the three coats on in succession. In this case, attach the keel to the hull as above, and lay masking tape on the hull flush to each side of the keel. Brush on one coat of epoxy. While the epoxy is still fresh, remove the tape, and let the epoxy sag gently into the crevice between hull and keel. When tacky, retape and repeat for a second coat of epoxy.

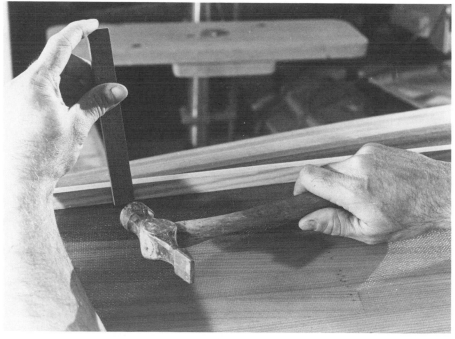

FINAL DETAILS

Adding the Finishing Touches

The creation of beauty is more satisfying and joyous than mere possession.
— *John Gardner*

Just as many a race is lost within eyeshot of the finish line, so, too, can a canoe-building project meet with disaster after the most demanding work has been done. When I relocated my own boatshop to a long-vacant old building in the village of Bancroft, Ontario, it was midwinter, and I was pressed to complete a client's Redbird canoe. The hull was built and trimmed; it only needed a few coats of varnish to be ready for delivery. Worried about the dust that had accumulated in the building during years of disuse, I painstakingly vacuumed and vacuumed again, sucking the dust from the floors, walls and windows. I then let the shop settle a day or two,

mindful that even a vacuum leaves a residue of particles hanging in the air. Confident that the workplace was clean, I fired up the woodstove and set to work. But as the drafty shop's temperature rose to a varnish-drying norm, hundreds of dormant flies began to stir to life, kicking themselves awake and swarming with delight to the toastiest spot in the room – the unvacuumed ceiling. Sadly, it was as the third coat of varnish was drying that I noticed the rain of dust beginning to drift down. Since thin coats of varnish are all-important and must be perfect to maintain a canoe's freshly built beauty, I resolutely sanded off the hull and started over again.

VARNISHING

Tools:

1½-to-3-inch foam brush
tack cloth
clean cloths

Materials:

varnish
solvent
sandpaper #220
disposable paint filter
wet sanding paper #240

Safety:

ventilation
dust mask

While most first-time builders view rocks and deadheads as the sworn enemies of their lustrous new hulls, it is, in fact, the sun that

can do the most damage to a new woodstrip/epoxy canoe. Curiously, in spite of the epoxy's tough surface, it takes a coating of varnish to prevent the sun's ultraviolet rays from breaking down the resin and turning it milky. And the varnish also protects the bare trim from water damage, while accentuating the highlights of the wood grain.

The hull is varnished with the seats and thwarts removed so you can reach the hull interior without obstruction. And if the decks are very long, the hull interior and deck undersides should be varnished before they are installed. (Each of the seats and thwarts is reinstalled only after a thorough varnishing.)

Varnish Room

The secret of a lasting varnish job is good equipment and generous doses of care and patience. Your work area must be clean, warm and dry, well ventilated and as dust-free as possible. Buy a disposable wedge-shaped foam brush for this job as bristle brushes shed and are expensive. Use a disposable paint filter to strain the varnish before brushing it on (even from a newly opened can).

Wipe down the surface with varnish solvent, then go over it carefully with a tack cloth to pick up any tiny particles left behind. Varnish the inside of the canoe first, one half at a time, dividing the hull down the keel-line. Do not neglect the crevices up under the decks or the undersides of the gunwales.

Soaking your brush with varnish, "float" the varnish on, brushing it gently and smoothly from wet to dry in the direction of the grain, being careful always to keep a wet edge. Let the first coat dry completely, following manufacturer's instructions.

Sand the entire surface lightly but thoroughly with #220 sandpaper, or wet-sand with #240. Clean with the recommended solvent, and wipe down with a tack cloth. Apply a second coat, let it dry, then sand again with #220 paper or fine steel wool. Clean the surface and brush on a third coat.

When the inside is dry, turn the canoe over, and varnish the exterior of the hull. Three coats are adequate, but of course, the more coats you apply, the tougher the shield — if you have six coats of varnish and a scratch gouges three, the hull is still well protected. I apply nine coats of varnish to the vintage mahogany runabouts that I restore, but five or six are probably the maximum justifiable on a woodstrip canoe. The trade-off you make for protection is weight: Each coat adds at least an extra pound.

One diligent builder brushed on five or six thin coats and then, after a final sanding, paid a car body shop $25 to spray on a flawless finish coat. As he admits, "It is hard not to get carried away when building these canoes."

PAINTING

For greater abrasion resistance, the outside of the hull can be painted, to the gunwales or just to the waterline.

Prepare the surface exactly as for varnishing. Select a marine linear polyurethane (LP) paint designed for use over epoxy. The two-part LP systems are light-, salt- and abrasion-resistant and bond extremely well to a cured resin surface. Apply two coats (following manufacturer's instructions), and sand between coats.

It may be difficult to bring yourself to cover the wood, even though you want the added resistance of paint. You can have the best of both by painting just to the four-inch waterline so the underside of the hull is protected, while the canoe above water is still obvi-

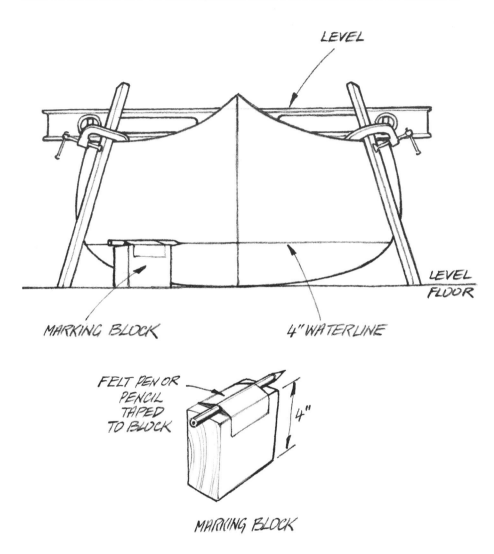

The difficulty in painting the underside of a canoe is keeping the painted edge straight. Find a level floor, and clamp "feet" to each gunwale amidships, adjusting them until the canoe is level. Then tape a pencil to a 4-inch block of wood and trace around the canoe, marking the waterline.

ously a woodstrip. To mark the waterline, set the canoe on a level floor, right side up. Stabilize it by clamping a stick to the outwales at amidships on either side, checking that the hull is perfectly level. Make up a marking block (as illustrated) and run it around the boat so the waterline is evenly traced.

Mark the bottom of this line with masking tape, and varnish the topsides. Avoid a hard edge by removing the tape just as the varnish begins to set, retaping for each of the second and third coats.

When the varnishing is complete, tape at the waterline so the paint will slightly overlap the varnish. Apply two coats, sanding and cleaning the surface between. Remove the tape before each coat is dry.

GRAPHITE FINISH

Graphite is a very fine black powder that, mixed with epoxy resin, produces a slippery, highly abrasion-resistant finish. The tough, low-friction surface is ideal for whitewater and wilderness canoes. WEST SYSTEM 406 Colodial Silica added to WEST SYSTEM 423 graphite powder will produce a rock-hard finish.

Prepare the hull as you would for painting to the waterline. Varnish the topsides first, then invert the hull and tape at the waterline so the graphite will overlap the varnish slightly.

Mix a batch of epoxy, adding up to 25 percent graphite powder and 5 percent Colodial Silica. Brush or

roll it on carefully, since it has a determined tendency to run.

When the graphite coat is rubbery, cut along the edge of the tape with a razor blade or sharp knife and peel it off. Do not remove the tape while the coat is runny, but do not wait until it is rock-hard.

For an even black matte finish, rub down the entire surface with very fine steel wool. It will come out as smooth as silk and as tough as steel.

STEM BAND

Tools:

drill/⅛-inch bit
screwdriver
file

Materials:

½-inch #4 noncorrosive flat head screws
½-inch #4 steel screws
bedding compound
stem band
painter ring

The stem band may seem superfluous, but it will save a great deal of wear and tear on the leading edge of your canoe. After one season in the water, the stem band will inevitably be scuffed and scratched, proof that it has been protecting your varnish job.

This metal strip normally covers the full length of the stem. If there is a keel, it is advisable to continue the band along its full length, stem to stem. On one wooden canoe that I restored, the unprotected keel was worn down ¼ inch below

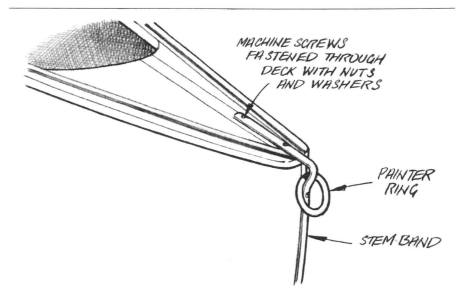

The leading edge of a canoe sustains the most wear and tear — protect it with a brass stem band fastened along the stem and keel.

the banded stem.

Drill and countersink the centre of the metal band at 5-inch intervals with a ⅛-inch bit, then place it on the stem. Use care in bending the metal, as it will want to crease first at the drilled holes.

The stem band is screwed in place with ½-inch #4 noncorrosive screws. Brass screw heads are notorious for twisting off under pressure, but you can avoid this by first twisting in a ½-inch #4 steel screw to cut the threads in the wood. Remove the steel and screw in the brass with a little silicone sealer or bedding compound on its tip. Be sure to countersink the head flush so it will not catch and rip out the screw. File down any rough edges.

Continue around the stem and

keel until the band is firmly in place. The metal should extend a couple of inches over the stems onto the deck. If you want a painter ring for tying lines onto, you can fasten the band with a raised eyelet to take the ring (see above). For more support, fasten the band at the end with machine screws that extend through the deck, secured with nuts and washers on the underside. Alternatively, drive the last screw ½ inch from the end of the band, and use an available fitting to attach the painter (see Sources, page 143).

As a final finishing touch, have a small brass plate engraved with the name of the boat, the date of first launching and the name of the builder. You now richly deserve this bit of recognition.

CLASSIC CARE
A Guide to Maintenance & Repair

Frailest of all crafts in which frail man ever set forth upon the waters of the world, the canoe is yet the one nearest perfection.

— *Marlow Shaw*

In 1877, Charles Hallock wrote in *The Sportsman's Gazeteer and General Guide*: "The first thing to find out about a boat is her age. Five years is about as old as is desirable under ordinary circumstances, as boats (as they are built nowadays) begin to get old when they pass this age."

Some of the canoes built when Hallock penned those words are still in active service today, long past their predicted prime. They have survived partly due to the way they were built but mostly because they have been intelligently used, properly stored and carefully maintained.

Woodstrip/epoxy construction eliminates many of the traditional problems associated with wood, but your canoe will nonetheless require some maintenance. Mostly, it demands good common sense — storing it so moisture does not contaminate the nonepoxied trim, transporting it so it stays on the roof rack and keeping the varnish intact. You may need to repair the scratches and scrapes that are an inevitable part of paddling, but as the builder, you put this craft together, so no repair is beyond your skills.

STORAGE

For a long life, this canoe should be stored with the same respect for the work that went into shaping those fair curves. Keep it dry, keep it level, and keep any weight off it. Store the boat indoors during the winter if possible, slung from the boathouse rafters or supported on a cradle. More than one owner of a woodstrip/epoxy canoe admits that his pride and joy spends the frozen months in a place of honour in the house, to be admired over the winter like a piece of fine furniture. But if outdoor storage is unavoidable, at least be sure that the canoe is covered and protected against the weight of heavy snow and falling trees.

In summer, always store the canoe out of the sun. If you are going to cover it with a tarp, be sure there is adequate air circulation around the hull to eliminate any heat or moisture build-up. And if you leave it outside, tie the canoe down so it does not blow away.

Each time the canoe is removed from the water, rinse any sand out of the inside, and wipe it down with a chamois inside and out. Store the canoe upside down, making sure no water is laying inside the decks. It is best to build a permanent rack on the wall of the garage or boathouse, padding it to preserve the gunwale finish, but if you must leave it overturned on the ground, set spacers under each stem and under the gunwales to keep the canoe away from ground moisture that could damage the trim.

CAR-TOPPING

The monocoque hull is much tougher than most people think, but bouncing off a car onto an

Centennial Museum, Peterborough

asphalt highway at 60 miles per hour is an unnecessary test of endurance. Learning proper "cartopping" techniques will not only prevent such disasters but save the finish from minor abrasions caused by rubbing ropes.

Fasten roof racks securely to the vehicle, padding them with carpet to protect the gunwales. Tie the canoe to *both* racks using stevedore's knots to winch the boat tightly against them.

Fasten the canoe to the front and back bumpers of the car in a three-point system that has ropes running from each end of the canoe to both sides of each bumper. The lines should be tight and should angle toward the midsection of the canoe, tied to the scuppers or thwarts, to counteract wind-force at the front and braking-force at the back, as well as to minimize the effect of crosswinds.

ROUTINE MAINTENANCE

The three to four coats of varnish you applied have a life span of at least three years on the outside and four to five years on the inside under average conditions, but the longevity of your boat will be extended considerably, with less effort, if you inspect it regularly. Check the bottom of the hull for scratches and the gunwales for wear from car racks or rubbing paddles. Be sure that the screws in the stem band and the nuts on the seats and thwarts are tight.

The frequency of maintenance depends on the amount of use and the exposure that the canoe is subjected to. Touch up scratches as they appear: When the finish starts to look scruffy from patching, re-varnish the hull.

The old varnish need not be stripped off to revive the finish. Lightly wet-sand the hull and trim with #320 paper to smooth the surface, removing the seats and thwarts to sand the inside. Clean off the hull with a solvent, wipe with a tack cloth, and apply fresh varnish using the same brand.

CARE IN THE WATER

Having built the canoe, you will undoubtedly have an acute interest in how it is used. For some, the creative process fosters an over-protectiveness toward their craft: "It is so beautiful that I have not yet launched it," reports one builder. For others, it is a release: "Building a canoe sets you free to really use it, knowing that if you do some damage, you can fix it."

As a paddler, you can put your complete confidence in the boat you have built. A woodstrip/epoxy canoe will withstand as much — or more — hard use than any other construction technique.

Anything will sustain damage when taken out of the medium in which it was designed to function. Avoid rocks and floating obstructions when possible. Be careful hauling the canoe up on the beach, and do not step into the hull unless it is resting on its cushion of water.

Ultimately, because scratches on the surface, deep cuts and even holes are easily repaired, the care you take in the water depends on your willingness to take the consequences of abuse.

REPAIR

Very few of the 200 Bear Mountain canoes built to date have ever sustained more than superficial damage, despite rigorous use. The construction method itself is highly durable, and when combined with the stiffening dome effect of good hull design (i.e., shallow arch, moderate rocker, slight tumblehome), these canoes will absorb and distribute incredible stress.

My most challenging repair was the result of an out-of-water accident. A spanking-new canoe, stoutly crated and en route to its new owner, was crushed in the boxcar by two tons of heavy equipment. The crate, a sturdy 1 x 2-inch frame covered with ⅜-inch particle board, looked like it had exploded, but the hull was intact, with only two cracks in the resin. The maple deck was split on one side: the glue joint held, but the hardwood fibres gave way and the #8 stainless steel screws were torn in half. This canoe was so successfully restored that it is difficult to imagine any stress that could push a woodstrip/epoxy canoe past the point of repair.

Loose Screws

If a screw is ripped out of the stem band, first plug the hole with a little piece of cedar dipped in epoxy glue. When you twist in a new screw, the fibres of the cedar will spread with the screw action, sealing out moisture.

Scratches in the Varnish

Minor surface wear most often appears on the outside of the hull bottom from bumping rocks, on the inside hull from the abrasive action of sand and sharp-edged gear, and on the gunwales from paddles and unpadded car racks.

On the hull, clean the scratches, and flow in a little varnish with a fine brush. On the gunwales, if the varnish is worn down to bare wood, repair the damage as soon as possible. If the wood has turned grey with exposure, sand down to a fresh colour, wet the wood to raise the fibres, and fine-sand again. Discoloured wood can also be restored to its natural hue by swabbing with a concentrated solution of oxalic acid. Varnish with a product compatible with the original, building up the layers.

Scratches in the Sheathing

A very sharp rock under considerable force might gouge a deep scratch into the resin, down to the glass but not the wood. To repair a resin scratch, sand the epoxy (using #80 sandpaper) about one inch in all directions around the damage, feathering out gradually. Do not sand deep enough to expose the wood. Protect the varnish on the rest of the canoe by masking off the area to be patched before you start to sand.

Cut a patch of fibreglass to cover the scratch, overlapping the feathered edge of the old cloth. Brush epoxy on the sanded surface, lay in the patch, and wet it out with a little more resin.

For a smooth one-coat finish, lay a piece of wax paper over the repair and squeegee, working out from the centre to remove excess air and resin. Let the patch cure, then peel off the wax paper. If you have been careful feathering and squeegeeing, the patch will be smooth and at the same level and density as the original sheath. If not, feather the edges, and brush on another coat of resin.

Sand the cured epoxy, and build up the varnish over the patch to match the hull. For an invisible repair, sand the entire hull lightly, and brush on a coat of varnish.

Scratches to the Wood Core

Begin as above but sand down to the wood. Remove any loose fibres, then fill the scratch with epoxy filler. Be sure to use fine sawdust that is a lighter colour than the planking so they will match when set up. Sand level with #80 sandpaper, wet down and fine-sand with #120 paper. If you neglect the wetting and second sanding, the patch will show up darker than the original planking. Proceed as above, laying in cloth, epoxy, then varnish.

Damage from a Blow

A blow from a rounded object may cause a slight dimple or dent that you can feel with your hand along the outside of the hull. If there are no other signs, there is likely no damage needing repair.

If the sheath goes white in one spot, it indicates that the cloth stretched slightly inside the resin. If the surface of the varnish is intact, the epoxy layer itself is probably unharmed and the glass unbroken. The hull is still waterproof, and repairs can wait until the end of the season; then restore as described above.

The blow may crack the glass and resin, especially along the grain of the wood on the side of the hull opposite the blow as damage is more likely to occur where the hull lets go in tension than where it is hit. If a crack is discovered, treat as a scratch in the sheathing.

After a violent blow to the hull, if there are no obvious breaks in the sheath, check for separation within the woodstrips, the weakest link in the monocoque structure. The fibres themselves may shear apart when the hull layers are stretched out of alignment. Press on the spot and tap it. If there is movement, if it feels spongy or if you hear a dulling of the normal wood resonance, the area needs repair. If the sheath is still watertight, there is no rush, though the process becomes complicated if moisture seeps in.

To repair the wood without disturbing the sheath, drill a ⅛-inch hole into the high side of the damaged spot, and mask off the area. With a syringe, squirt heated resin into the void. Warm the hull with a hot-air gun so the resin will be as runny as possible, seeping into all the cracks. When cured, sand smooth and varnish.

If the blow breaks the resin and glass and cracks a plank, sand down to the wood. Take out any loose fibres, and try to fit the plank back together. If it can still be forced into position, spread the break, coat all surfaces with epoxy glue, and press the plank back into shape. Secure the strip in position with duct tape. It is important to retain the curvature of the original core. If the break is at a difficult point, and the repair wants to pop out, tie ropes around the hull, and force wedges between the ropes and the glued plank to hold it firm as it sets. When the epoxy is cured, sand the wood smooth, wet to raise the fibres, and sand again. Finish as for a scratch.

Even though it is almost inconceivable that a hull could be so badly damaged that the wood itself became irreparable, it would still be readily fixable. First, you remove the damaged section so that there is only sound wood around the perimeter of the hole. (Avoid the temptation of cutting out a square or rectangle, and aim for a more irregular shape that will produce a stronger bond and be less obvious.) Then, after feathering the edges of the fibreglass and epoxy in preparation for patching, take several wooden strips, and begin planking over top of the hole on the outside of the hull (being careful to align the edges of the new planking with that of the rest of the hull), extending these new strips well over the hole onto the solid hull. After gluing enough repair strips together to cover the hole, tape the oversized patch to the hull, and let the glue dry.

Once the glue has dried, you have the basis of a patch that, while bigger than the actual puncture, has been constructed to take the same curve as the hull. To give this custom patch extra strength, add some fibreglass cloth and one coat of epoxy to it, and leave to dry. When it is set, trace the shape of the hole from inside the hull so that you can remove the patch from the hull and cut it to shape. Then set the patch into the hole.

Sand and lay up the patch on the inside, extending the glass over the cut edges. On the outside, lay a strip of cloth around the perimeter of the patch to bond the repair to the original hull. Continue building up the epoxy to the same thickness and density as the original, and finish as above.

If you are unable to find matching wood strips for the repair (you may wish to save a few pieces from the original batch for just such an unlikely occasion), make the best of a bad situation by cutting the damage out in a design shape, and fill it with contrasting wood. It may look as if you did the inlay as an artistic fillip.

SOURCES

GENERAL SUPPLIERS

The following are the most prominent known sources for canoe woods, hardware, accessories and kits. Your nearest boatbuilder will also be an invaluable font of information and will probably be able to direct you to the best local suppliers.

Cedarglas Canoe Ltd.
9 Allaura Blvd.
#10
Aurora, Ontario
L4G 3N2
Canoe kits and parts.

Alex Comb
Route 1, Box 319
Two Harbors, Minnesota
55616
Bronze, brass, stainless steel hardware, accessories (gunwales, decks, seats, yokes, thwarts, paddles).

Duck Trap Woodworking
R.F.D. 2, Cannan Road
Lincolnville Beach, Maine
04849
Plans for three lapstrake canoes (not adapted for woodstrip/epoxy construction), sail plan, white cedar, fastenings, mast fittings.

Freedom Boat Works
Route 1, Box 12
North Freedom, Wisconsin
53951
Sailing rigs.

Old Town Canoe Co.
58 Middle Street
Old Town, Maine
04468
Woodstrip canoe kit, wood, accessories.

Rice Creek Boat Works
9715 Jackson Street NE
Blaine, Minnesota
55434
Woodstrip canoe kits, plans, red cedar, epoxy, fibreglass cloth, sail rig plans and kit, accessories, including seats.

Tendercraft Boat Shop
67 Mowat Avenue
Toronto, Ontario
M6K 3E3
Planking (bead-and-cove), seats, hardware, fibreglass supplies, sailing rigs, brass stem band, varnish, paint, books, tools.

Willis Enterprises Inc.
Curtis Road R.D. 3, Box 114A
Freeport, Maine
04032
Woodstrip canoe kit, planking, safety supplies, canoe plans, books, accessories, paddles.

HARDWARE

Paxam Metals
5225 Timberlea Blvd.
Mississauga, Ontario
L4W 2S3
Brass stem banding.

Majestic Fasteners
Box 193
Morris Plains, New Jersey
07950
Bronze and brass bolts and screws (minimum order $25).

FIBREGLASSING MATERIALS, VARNISH, PAINTS

Whorwood Enterprises
580 Quebec Street
London, Ontario
N5W 3Z2
Handles WEST SYSTEM products. Will ship direct anywhere in Canada or advise of local distributor.

Gougeon Brothers Inc.
706 Martin Street
Bay City, Michigan
48706
Handles WEST SYSTEM products. Will ship direct in the United States or advise of local distributor.

PADDLE BLANKS

Ray Kettlewell
167 Burns St.
Strathroy, Ontario
N7G 1E7
Paddle blanks and paddles.

PADDLES

Grassmere Paddles
Box 658
Bracebridge, Ontario
P0B 1C0

Grey Owl Paddles
101 Sheldon Drive
Cambridge, Ontario
N1R 6T6

Nimbus Paddles Ltd.
2330 Tyner St., Unit 6
Port Coquitlam, British Columbia
V3C 2Z1

Shaw & Tenney
P.O. Box 213J
Orono, Maine
04473

PLANS

The Bear Mountain Boat Shop
Box 1041
Bancroft, Ontario
K01 1C0

Mrs. R.D. Culler
85 Cedar Street
Hyannis, Massachusetts
02601
Sells plans for Pete Culler's 12-foot 9-inch Butternut plus a 17-foot model (not adapted for woodstrip/epoxy construction).

Minnesota Canoe Association
P.O. Box 14207
University Station
Minneapolis, Minnesota
55414
Sells plans for 10 woodstrip/resin canoes from 13-foot 6-inch white-water solo to 30-foot club canoe, to members only ($10/year).

Mystic Seaport Museum Inc.
Mystic, Connecticut
06355
Attention: Boat Lines, Curatorial Department
Sells lines, offset table, construction plan and sail plan for variety of traditional paddling and sailing canoes (not adapted for woodstrip/epoxy construction).

United States Canoe Association
Larry Hampel
15 South 12th Street
St. Charles, Illinois
60174
Sells full-scale plans for woodstrip/resin canoes in 4 models: C-1, C-2, C-4 and 18-foot 6-inch cruiser.

National Sailing Committee
American Canoe Association
P.O. Box 248
Lorton, Virginia
22079
Distributes plans of canoe sailing rigs and instructions on how to build them. ACA newsletter *Downeast Sailor* lists sources for sailing rigs and parts.

TOOLS

Furnima Industrial Carbide
P.O. Box 308
Barry's Bay, Ontario
K0J 1B0
Only distributor for carbide bead-and-cove cutters for router. Plans for jig included.

Lee Valley Tools Ltd.
P.O. Box 6295, Stn. J
Ottawa, Ontario
K2A 1T4

Garrett Wade Co.
161 Avenue of the Americas
New York, New York
10013

Woodcraft Supply Corp.
41 Atlantic Avenue
P.O. Box 4000
Woburn, Massachusetts
01888

CANOE ORGANIZATIONS

Canadian Canoe Association
333 River Road
Vanier City, Ontario
K1L 8B9

American Canoe Association
7217 Lockport Place
Box 248
Lorton, Virginia
22079

Traditional Small Craft Association
Box 350
Mystic, Connecticut
06355

United States Canoe Association
15 South 12th Street
St. Charles, Illinois
60174

Wooden Canoe Heritage Association Ltd.
P.O. Box 5634
Madison, Wisconsin
53705

Note: Most of these national organizations publish a newsletter and will be able to put you in contact with local chapters.

PERIODICALS

Canadian Yachting
425 University Avenue, 6th Floor
Toronto, Ontario
M5G 1T6

Canoe
(formerly American Canoeist)
Voyageur Publications Inc.
1204 W. Main Street
Fort Wayne, Indiana
46808

National Fisherman
Journal Publications
21 Elm Street
Camden, Maine
04843

Woodenboat
Box 78
Brooklin, Maine
04616

Small Boat Journal
P.O. Box 400
Bennington, Vermont
05201

Wilderness Camping
(annual canoe issue)
1597 Union St.
Schenectady, New York
12309

CANOE MUSEUMS

Adirondack Museum
Blue Mountain Lake,
New York
12812

Thousand Islands Shipyard Museum
750 Mary Street
Clayton, New York
13624

Mystic Seaport Museum
Mystic, Connecticut
06355

Kanawa Canoe Museum
Dorset, Ontario
P0A 1E0

The Mariners Museum
Newport News, Virginia

REFERENCES

Canoe Design

Evans, Eric, "Canoes According to Galt," *Small Boat Journal*

(June/July 1982)
Mike Galt's outspoken views on what is wrong with contemporary canoes, how they got that way, and how to improve them.

Hankins, D., "Design – The Long and the Short of It," *Down River* (March 1977)

Sehlinger, B., "Canoe Design," *Down River* (August 1977)

La Brant, Howie, "The Principles of Canoe Design," *American White Water Journal* (Autumn 1962). Excellent overview of basic elements of design and their interplay.

Brewer, Edwards and Betts, Jim, *Understanding Boat Design.* Camden, Maine, International Marine, 1980

Herreshoff, L. Francis, *Sensible Cruising Designs.* Camden, Maine, International Marine, 1973

Boatbuilding

Chapelle, Howard, *American Small Sailing Craft.* New York, Norton, 1951 Extensive, detailed instructions for backyard builders including 100 plans for sailboats under 40 feet.

Chapelle, Howard, *Boatbuilding.* New York, Norton, 1941 Complete handbook of wooden boat construction.

Gardner, John, *Building Classic Small Craft.* Camden, Maine

International Marine, 1977 Inspiration for builders interested in the best of small boats of the past.

Gilpatrick, Gil, *Building a Strip Canoe.* Yarmouth, Maine DeLorme Publishers, 1979 Instructions for woodstrip/polyester resin canoes including plans for five models.

Gougeon, *The Gougeon Brothers on Boat Construction*, 1979. Gougeon Bros. Inc. Bay City, Michigan Describes WEST SYSTEM of cold-moulding in wood using epoxy resin.

Hazen, David, *The Stripper's Guide to Canoe Building.* Larkspur, California Tamal Vista, 1982 One of the first woodstrip/polyester resin construction manuals. Includes plans for several canoes and kayaks.

Ketter, Karl, *How to Build a Canoe.* Minneapolis, Minnesota Minnesota Canoe Association, Ltd., 1968

Rabl, S.S., *Boatbuilding in Your Own Backyard.* Ithaca, New York Cornell Maritime Press, 1958 One of the best boatbuilding books directed at the amateur. Discusses wood, tools and lofting.

Roberts, Harry N., "On Canoe Construction," *Wilderness Camping Magazine* (1978 annual)

Excellent overview of the rationale for and the strengths and weaknesses of various materials, and the construction methods associated with them.

Culler, R.D., *Boats, Oars and Rowing.* Camden, Maine International Marine. Includes plans for a double-paddle canoe, sprit-rigging and oar-making.

Lofting

Vaitses, Alan, *Lofting.* Camden, Maine International Marine, 1980. The only available text devoted strictly to lofting. Discusses basic concepts as well as specific requirements of different hull types.

Paddles

American Red Cross, *Canoeing.* New York, Doubleday, 1977. Discusses paddle design, some history and instruction for making a single-blade paddle.

Herreshoff, L. Francis, *Sensible Cruising Designs.* Camden, Maine International Marine, 1973. Includes Herreshoff double-blade paddle design.

Blandford, Percy, *Canoes and Canoeing.* New York W.W. Norton & Co., 1968. Discusses paddle-making for British covered canoes.

Ellis, Alec R. and Beams, C.G. *How to Build & Manage a Canoe.* Glasgow Brown & Son & Ferguson, 1975. Volume 2 describes paddle-making techniques.

Stelmok, Jerry, *Building the Maine Guide Canoe.* Camden, Maine International Marine, 1980. Discusses paddle-making techniques for single blade.

Sailing

Gardner, John, "Sailing Canoes Once Held a Brief Place in the Sun," *National Fisherman* (June 1977).

Miller, Lew, "How to Sail a Stripper," *Canoe* (June 1978)

Manning, Sam, "Sticks and String," *Woodenboat* (May 1978)

Paulson, F.M., "Canoe Sailing Rigs," *Field and Stream* (August 1966)

"Sailing Rig for Redwood Canoe," *Popular Science* (August 1970)

The following books, listed elsewhere in the bibliography, also have chapters devoted to rigging a canoe for sail:

American National Red Cross, *Canoeing.*
Chapelle, Howard, *American Small Sailing Craft.*
Blandford, Percy W., *Canoes & Canoeing.*
Stelmok, Jerry, *Building the Maine Guide Canoe.*

Ted Moores and his partner Joan Barrett are known across North America for their canoebuilding and wooden-boat restoration. Their Bear Mountain Boat Shop is based in Bancroft, Ontario.

Merilyn Mohr lives outside North Bay, Ontario, with her husband and two children. A regular contributor to *Harrowsmith* magazine, she is the author of *The Art of Soapmaking*.

ACKNOWLEDGEMENTS

Our first thank you goes to the many builders of Bear Mountain canoe kits and to the countless backyard boat builders whose enthusiasm and persistence inspired the writing of this book.

We appreciate the assistance of the many experts who took an interest in this project and gave us the benefit of their expertise, especially the late Dr. Donald Cameron, canoe historian; John Gardner, Associate Curator of Small Craft at Mystic Seaport; Kirk Whipper and the Kanawa Canoe Museum; Jan Gougeon, one of the developers of the WEST SYSTEM; Bill Mason, author, film maker and paddler par excellence; the descendants of Daniel Herald, Walter Dean, Thomas Gordon and John Stephenson; amateur builders M.E. Walker and Richard Barlow; Walter Walker, canoe builder; Fred Johnston of the Canadian Canoe Association; and the librarians and archivists who patiently assisted us in our searches.

— *Merilyn Mohr*
Ted Moores